HOUSEHOLD
BAGGAGE
HANDLERS

EDITED BY
M A R N A   A S H B U R N
Author of *Household Baggage*

HOUSEHOLD
BAGGAGE
HANDLERS

56 STORIES
FROM THE HEARTS AND LIVES
OF MILITARY WIVES

Wyatt-MacKenzie Publishing
D E A D W O O D ,   O R E G O N

Household Baggage Handlers
56 Stories from the Hearts and Lives of Military Wives, 2nd Ed
Marna Ashburn

Wyatt-MacKenzie Publishing
DEADWOOD, OREGON

www.WyattMacKenzie.com

Requests for permission or further information should be addressed to:
Wyatt-MacKenzie Publishing
15115 Highway 36, Deadwood, Oregon 97430

Printed in the United States of America

DEDICATION

To my children, still my greatest teachers.

No one ever warned me
When I became a military wife
About all the challenges
I'd have to face in my life.

No one ever told me
And that's a good thing
For I may have turned and run
And missed out on this ring.

This ring that encircles
My sister military wives
It holds us together
And joins our lives.

From "No One Ever Told Me" by Joy Kovacevic

Joy Kovacevic is an Army wife and mother of two boys, Michael and Nathan. In addition to her own family, Joy is devoted to her Army family and volunteers whenever asked in the hopes of making Army life better for her husband's fellow soldiers and their families.

Contents

Introduction i

MOVING PORTRAITS

Moving Schizophrenia by Susanna Hickman Bartee 2
"Hey, Where's Your TV?" by Ally Rodriguez 4
How to Adapt and Overcome With Moves by Shannon Croteau . 8
Hazmat Vehicles and the Art of Ziplocs by Janine Boldrin. 12
Grace by Valerie H. Adams 15
The Pre-Move Adventure by Laura Ornelas 17
Moving Again and Again by Christie Morgans. 23
Strangers Packing My Underwear Drawer by Suzie Trotter . . . 26

NORMAL, OR SOMETHING LIKE IT

My Kind of Normal by Sonya Mooneyham 30
You Know You're a Military Wife When by Sarah Smiley 33
The Greatest Good by Ruthie Alekseyev 36
Live It, Breathe It, Blow It Up by René Lowe 39
The DITY Gazebo by Lee Anne Gallaway-Mitchell 41

KEEPING IT TOGETHER (BARELY)

Pickles and the US Navy by Desireé Colvin 46
Taxing the Wife Martha Merritt 48
Sickest Child by Sarah Smiley 51
The Easy Life by Suzie Trotter 54

A FUNNY THING HAPPENED ON THE WAY

A Change of Life by Betty Packard 60
Dress Mess by Janine Boldrin 63
Tacos With a Side Order of Foot-in-the-Mouth by Anna Gibbons 65
It's All About the Dress by Linda Eberharter 68
Queen of Everything by Ellie Kay 71

CATS AND BATS

He's Thinking Arby's by Tara Crooks 76

Blame It on Rio by Nora Carman 80

I Can Handle Just About Anything But That by Andi Hurley . 84

Critter Jitters by Janine Boldrin 87

Cats on a Plane by Angela Owens 89

WEIRD WEATHER WE'RE HAVING

It Was a Dark and Stormy Night by Phyllis Denton 96

The Safest Aisle in the Commissary by Lisa Sweet. 99

Winter in Alaska with a Toddler by Heather L. Ward 102

Dodging Bullets by Jacey Eckhart 106

FAMILY PLANNING, MILITARY STYLE

Unexpected Strength by Deborah Logan Horstkotte 110

My Brilliant Life Plan by Phyllis Denton 114

Michael's Story by Lisa Glen 119

It's in the Water by Kelly Pike 124

Special Delivery at Gate Five by Mary Beth Smith 127

FRIENDS, FAMILY, AND EVERYTHING IN BETWEEN

Flying Solo by Martha Merritt 132

Wanted: New Best Friend by Wendy Barrett 134

Becoming Family by Devin Patton 136

The Family Forge by Terri Barnes 140

VIETNAM AND EARLIER VINTAGES

Flexible From the Beginning by Carole France 144

Letters From Vietnam by Judy Hunt Rudolph 147

Many Good Men by Nancy Denton 151

The Road Taken by Bonnie Leonard 155

A Great Trip Together by Louise Smith 159

CONSIDERING LOSS

The Little Manila Envelope by Andi Hurley. 164

Sorority Sisters by Susan Hood Franz. 166

Will I See You Tomorrow? by Phyllis Ward 169

A Few Terrifying Moments by Kris Johnson 174

HOME, HEARTH, AND HOLIDAYS

The Incredible Shrinking Quarters by Shella Farrell 180
Hooah Chic by Angela Owens 184
December During Deployments by Marna Ashburn 187
Collecting and Creating Traditions by Kathie Hightower . . 190

MOVING ON

A Loud Silence by Suzie Trotter 196
Missing It by Mary Cornell 200
Yes, Virginia, There Is an Afterlife by Joan Brown 203

Gratitude 207
About the Illustrator 208

Introduction

"We are the ones who embrace emotions,
who collect the leftover crumbs of seemingly meaningless
days, who touch on the cycles of life and remember
what happened in our families."

FROM *PEONY IN LOVE* BY LISA SEE

After my book, *Household Baggage: The Moving Life of a Military Wife*, was published in 2006, military wives across the country emailed their stories to me—tragic, comic, and everything in between. The wit and wisdom of this remarkable group convinced me the tales belonged in a collection for others to read and enjoy. Many responded to my invitation to write down their memorable military moments, and the result is *Household Baggage Handlers*, which is much more than an anthology. With such an array of styles, emotions, and experiences, it's more like a chat with sisters who've been on the same journey.

MARNA ASHBURN, *Editor*

Moving Portraits

Moving Schizophrenia
SUSANNA HICKMAN BARTEE

I love moving. I think it's exciting to scope out our potential new digs in whatever place the Army is sending us next. My husband has no sooner waved new orders at me than I am Googling the place and looking at real estate. Never mind that the house of our dreams (six-bedroom, four-bath with a screened-in porch) is beyond our budget no matter where in the world we might live. This is still the planning stage so I get to dream that we might actually live in that fabulous house. I just love moving.

I hate moving. Reality has forced its way in and we are, in fact, moving to a four-bedroom, two-bath, no-screened-in porch house. Pooh. I keep hoping for a miracle and that we will pass a huge, new home just as we are nearing our new duty station. And it will have a sign out front: "Desperate to rent—large families receive a discount." That doesn't happen. Pooh again. I hate moving.

I love moving. Fitting our furniture into a new space is just like solving a life-size, 3D jigsaw puzzle. Husband gets points for moving the sleeper sofa four times until I find exactly the right spot. Kids get points for tossing out all those broken toys and playing with the ones they have unpacked as if it is Christmas morning. I get points for finding the perfect lace curtains *on sale* at Wal-Mart. It's sort of like playing doll-house on a really huge scale. Even our old stuff looks a little like new after it's rearranged. I love moving.

I hate moving. All of this unpacking has produced a ton and a half of cardboard dust. And where did all these stupid knick-knacks come from? Why can my husband find his golf tees with no problem but I am pulling hot pizza out of the oven with paper towels because the mitts seem to have disappeared? Forget my great plans of pristine organization. Now I am just shoving stuff into any closet that still has room. I'll sort it all out later. Maybe. I hate moving.

I love moving. I couldn't find a decent Bunko group to save my life at the last place. Now I have both Bunko and book club too. Wow! The women here are great. It's like we're all long-lost sisters. Even our kids get along. Anytime I feel lonely I can step outside and find a friend waiting to chat. Someone brought over coffeecake this morning and another neighbor is planning "Girls Night Out!" I love moving.

I hate moving. These people are driving me crazy. I can't even step outside my door without having a long conversation with one neighbor or another. And it seems there are constantly kids in my house WHO AREN'T MINE! Not a day goes by that someone doesn't come knocking on my door. So much for my weekly "pajama day." I hate moving.

I love moving. There's something about a clean slate that makes me eager to try anything new. I would never have signed up for ballroom dancing or tried teaching Sunday School at the old place. I would never have thought to use that old nightstand in the living room as an end table, but I love the way it looks in there. I would never have actually printed that chore chart and put it on the fridge, but the kids are slowly learning how to help out more around here. And, Lord knows, I would never have started jogging if not for my neighbor up the street and her ability to tell a story that pushes me for another half-mile. I love moving.

I hate moving. New orders just arrived. This place that feels like home will soon be another memory packed away to make room for something new. The kids are whining about leaving their friends. I'm whining about leaving mine. There's not enough time to have a yard sale and I haven't heard anything good about where we're going. Yeesh, I hate moving.

Then again, I wonder what six bedrooms are going for there?

SUSANNA HICKMAN BARTEE is the wife of a retired Army officer, a mother of six, and a real estate broker living near Fort Leavenworth, Kansas. She loves to write in what little spare time she finds.

"Hey, Where's Your TV?"
ALLY RODRIGUEZ

I had mixed emotions as the packers rummaged through my cupboards, wrapping dishes and cups in thick paper. My time had come—the end of my service with the U.S. Army. I was happy it was all over, yet sad and lost because not only was the Army my job, it was my life. I started thinking, "This is just the end of another chapter." In a few months, I'd be moving to Fort Riley, Kansas, to welcome my husband back from a 15-month tour in Iraq.

"Mrs. Rodriguez, do you want this stuffed penguin in the box?"

"Yes," I said. "I want everything packed." I ran from room to room, making sure these ladies, whom I'd never met, were being careful with my things. The two women—one middle-aged, stocky woman who seemed to enjoy her job and an awkwardly thin young woman in her early twenties who thoroughly hated her job—worked quickly yet efficiently. In two hours, they had packed my entire house and organized it into what looked like 100 various-sized boxes.

Then the movers showed up—three guys who looked like they'd rather be smoking some illegal substance than helping move my furniture. All three were in their mid-twenties and did not hide the fact that they hated their jobs. The taller of the three apparently had a "thing" for the young packer, because he kept trying to ask her on a date. The other two chain-smoked and carried on inappropriate conversations in front of me. Eventually, they began moving boxes and baggage until everything was on the truck.

"Mrs. Rodriguez," said the older lady, "can you look over the paperwork with me so I can explain all this to you?"

"Sure," I said, relieved that these strangers were getting out of my house. As I shuffled paperwork, signing here and initialing there, the lady asked how the movers did. "Great!" I replied. "They did well. I'm pleased." I signed the last bit of paperwork and off everyone went. I waved goodbye, shouted a big "Thanks!" and went inside. My stuff was headed for storage for six months until my husband came back from Iraq and I moved to Fort Riley.

Doing some last minute cleaning, I opened the cupboards, and ate every compliment that had just come out of my mouth. All of my plates, bowls, and drinking glasses, were still there! I opened the drawers and all of my utensils were there, too! The little old packing lady had only packed a few mugs, some glasses and a plate or two. I went upstairs and found that my entire bathroom set hadn't even been touched. I screamed. What was I supposed to do with all of this stuff?

Because I was driving from Virginia to Massachusetts to stay with my parents for a while, I had limited room in my car. I decided the only thing I could do was throw everything on the sidewalk. So I took my trash bin, which was also left behind, and filled it with the rest of my plates, glasses and silverware. Then I went upstairs, grabbed my bathroom set, and put that on the sidewalk, too. Two days later everything was gone, and it wasn't even trash day! It made me smile to imagine another family enjoying our dishes.

I moved back with my parents in Massachusetts until my husband finished his deployment. Six months later, I received a phone call saying my household stuff would arrive the next day.

When the truck pulled up, two young men got out. I greeted them with a smile and a handshake. They looked at me with a sense of aggravation and impatience. Then the driver, an older gentleman with thinning gray hair and a warm smile, stepped out, and shook my hand.

"Ms. Ally, it's nice to meet you. Let's get to work!" I was so excited I couldn't stop smiling! I was *finally* getting my stuff back!

Box-by-box they began unloading the massive truck and hauling my things into the storage shed in my parents' back yard. It was a frigid November night, so I asked my mother to make the men some coffee. She quickly returned with coffee and cookies. As the men ate we chatted about the Army, Iraq,

Boston and how much junk belonged to the next delivery. "Well, back to work!" the driver said. The two young men looked at each other; one mumbled something so unpleasant I dare not write it down.

"189, ma'am," someone called out a box number.

"Check," I replied.

"167," another shouted.

"Oh, that's my stuffed penguin!" I said cheerfully.

Two hours passed, and they finished. I looked down at the paperwork and said, "Hey guys, a few boxes are missing."

"Not a problem. We'll find them." The driver seemed sure of it. The two young men rolled their eyes. They did not love their job. I looked at the unchecked numbers on the inventory sheet and saw that my computer, monitor, webcam, microphone, and everything I had on my desk were missing. Suddenly, I felt a knot grow in my throat. I wanted to cry, but I held the tears back. Maybe I just forgot to check off the box numbers?

The driver suggested we go to the shed and recall the numbers. We did, twice. Then I really started to cry. I didn't cry because my computer was stolen—I could buy another one. I cried because I had stored precious photographs of my baby daughter on it. There were also pictures of my Army career, my husband and I when we were dating, and pictures of a Battle Buddy of mine who made the ultimate sacrifice. But most importantly, I'd miss the photos of my baby girl.

"Hey Ma'am, where's your TV? We didn't bring it in, did we?"

I scanned the paperwork, and sure enough, my television was among the unchecked items.

"You gotta be kidding me!?"

The driver looked at my paperwork, then looked me straight in the eyes and said, "Mrs. Rodriguez, I've been doing this for 27 years. I can just look at something and know it ain't right. Your living room was the first room to be put on the truck, so how come your TV, computer, and monitor were the last things to be loaded? Ma'am, this was planned."

The knot in my throat grew tighter. I couldn't believe it!

After I had been so nice to the packers and the original moving crew! After I helped them load the truck! Even after I gave one of the girls my suede coat, they did me dirty! I felt sick.

The driver explained how to file a claim and apologized about a dozen times and told me that XYZ Company was under investigation and probation for countless similar incidents. Probation! I wasn't the first, and probably not the last, yet this company was still dealing with service members. Unbelievable!

The next morning, I called the claims number only to be passed from one company to another. Finally, I contacted someone who told me to mail in my pink slip, and she'd send me a packet instructing me on the proper procedures to file a claim.

I'm still waiting for that packet. Recently, I filed a claim with my personal renter's insurance company. It, too, is a long and frustrating process.

After sharing my story with my friend Kelly Bedwell stationed at Schofield Barracks, Hawaii, she said, "What I do is make them give me their employee number, then I call the company to verify that all the people in my house that day belonged there. In three PCS moves, I've never had anything stolen."

A warning to all service members and families: double checking with the agency isn't a bad idea. Also, storing copies of precious pictures on a thumb drive, or even printing them the old-fashioned way, is a good idea. Remember to do a walk-through to confirm the packers got everything. Learn from my story so you aren't left with the same heartaches and hassles.

ALLY RODRIGUEZ is a former Signal Support Systems Specialist in the Army. She and her husband, SFC (RET) Gus Rodriguez have been married 11 years and have four children. Ally works for the Commonwealth of Massachusetts as a Disabled Veterans Outreach Program Specialist, where she helps disabled Veterans enter the workforce. She is currently earning a Master of Arts in Organizational Leadership.

How to Adapt and Overcome with Moves
SHANNON CROTEAU

"Honey, I have some news about my next duty station."

These are words every military wife both dreads and anticipates. When my call came in the early spring of 2000, I was 22 years old, just finished with my enlistment, had one baby at home and was pregnant with a second. Our next assignment was Darmstadt, Germany, a large base near the French border. I was excited because it was our first move from Fort Jackson, South Carolina, where my husband Nate and I had met, married, and started our family.

I had heard the Do's and Don't's of a big overseas move like this one and planned to be well prepared. I arranged for the movers to pick up our household goods three months before our expected arrival date of Memorial Day weekend. (Those of you who have been with the military long enough know they love to move soldiers during holidays!) I shipped our vehicle eight weeks before the move, and we rented a car until it was time to go. I was seven months pregnant and chasing a twelve-month old who had just learned to walk. Two days before the move, we got a call: we were being rerouted to a posting in Southern Germany, a place called Bad Aibling.

So off we went, sort of. We started with connecting flights in Columbia, South Carolina; Atlanta Georgia; London, England; Frankfurt, Germany; and then finally, Munich! However, there was no one to greet us at the airport, no USO, and we had no idea how to use a German pay phone. Three hours later, our sponsor showed up to take us to Bad Aibling via the Autobahn, which may not necessarily be scary in itself, but when you figure in a driver chirping on her cell phone while swerving through lanes, and talking to us, all at 150 kilometers per hour, it got pretty scary!

After this 27-hour journey, we arrived on post to hear some good news. Housing was available, and we were able to sign for it that day! The best news was that it was a first floor apartment in a stairwell building. The next best news was that it had been unnecessary to ship our household goods so early, because in overseas assignments, the post lends furniture and other items to waiting families. This turned out to be a good thing because our household goods got lost somewhere in England and didn't arrive until July, taking a full six months to reach us.

When the goods arrived (one of the most exciting days in my life) it looked as if T-Rex had attacked our furniture. Since we had only been married a short time before the move, our belongings were brand new. When I unpacked, I found broken televisions, bookcases ripped in half, and cracked dishes. It was awful. We called the legal assistant who had us write up the damages. We estimated about $3900 worth. While the claim was processed we made due with what we had. About a year later we got word: because it was such a large amount an adjustor needed to inspect the damages. We didn't have the items anymore; the legal person had said it was okay to throw the broken things out. We never saw a dime of reimbursement.

When it was time to leave Germany three years later, I was ready to take on those dinosaurs that ate furniture! I took pictures of everything we owned, turned on and off, to prove they worked. I videotaped the items next to newspapers to show they were working on a date just before packing. I would be ready this time.

We were sent to Fort Gordon, Georgia, where our goods arrived in just three weeks! I anticipated the same or similar damage but was surprised to find not one broken thing and not a scratch on the furniture! We had a good moving experience.

The next move took us to Fort Drum, New York, and again I took pictures and made my videotape, just in case. This time, our desk was broken, and there were several things missing from the truck, like my son's mattress set. I had the driver sign on the missing and damaged items, and filed my claim that day. I kept the broken furniture in my garage for seven months just in case, but when the claim came, they didn't need to see the furniture. The Army reimbursed me $35 because I didn't have receipts. I had no idea that I would need to keep receipts for all of my big purchase items, so I learned the hard way. The brand new desk and mattress alone cost $400!

So here are my lessons to help you have as stress-free a move as possible, whether it's across town or across the world:

- Find out if your new duty station has temporary furniture to loan, especially a washer and dryer. Most overseas assignments will provide these, which will allow you to keep your own items on hand until the last minute.

- Take pictures of everything turned on and off, like TVs and computers. This is to show that the item in question works when it's turned on, and shows its condition when turned off.

- Take a videotape of your items before the move showing their condition.

- Keep your own copy of a household inventory. Take advantage of the many mobile apps which allow you to organize your inventory into rooms and will even let you upload photos of your items.

- Get a three-ring binder with page protectors, and in the front place a copy of your household inventory. Every time you purchase something that costs over a certain dollar amount, (for me, it's $50) stick the receipt in there along with the warranty information and a photo of the product. Categorize your binder by room and update it often. This will save a lot of time if anything is broken or lost. All you have to do is pull out your receipt and your product information page.

- If there is a missing or damaged item, make sure you have the driver or person in charge of the move confirm it with a signature.

- If you have any damaged items, don't throw them out until your claim has been paid.

- If your spouse can't be there for the move, insist that the movers unload slowly enough for you to keep up. Often they shout out box or item numbers and you don't get a chance to make sure you are being told the right thing. Don't be afraid to tell them to slow down!

- Most importantly, purchase renter's insurance. Frequently it's too much of a hassle and a waste of time to get reimbursed through the military. Renter's insurance will cover you in government housing and during your moves. The rates are pretty inexpensive, ranging from $100-$200 a year. It's a small price to pay for peace of mind when it comes to your belongings.

Although there are bad moving experiences and good moving experiences, it all falls under the job description of a military spouse. By being prepared, things *can* go pretty smoothly! We just arrived in Hawaii and upon receiving our household goods, I overheard a mover say to his buddy, "This was the worst packing and shipping company I've ever come across." He was right. The list of broken and damaged items was extensive, but because I had my detailed records, I didn't stress, and was able to quickly file a claim through the Judge Advocate's Office. That's my way to "adapt and overcome."

SHANNON CROTEAU is married to her Army soldier Nate and has two children, Abbey and Tyler. An Army Reservist and self-proclaimed "scrapbookaholic," she's currently enrolled in a Master's of Education program.

Hazmat Vehicles and the Art of Ziplocs
JANINE BOLDRIN

The list of stuff movers will not transport often leaves me frustrated. Candles, paint, and batteries are just a few of the contraband items removed as the packers rummage through our house. Leaving these household goods behind gets expensive, since the Army likes to change our scenery at least once every three years.

In order to save money, my husband and I have devised an intricate plan that has served us well over the past four moves. We move the liquids and other hazardous items ourselves.

When we first looked at everything we needed to transport, it seemed overwhelming. But now we routinely gather up the motor oil, bug sprays, detergent bottles, window washer fluid, paint, antifreeze, and other larger bottles into boxes and load them into my husband's truck. Affectionately called the "Hazmat Vehicle," my husband has transported his precious cargo over many miles.

Although this works well for larger items, movers will also not take smaller liquid items either. Who could live without her extensive collection of Yankee Candles? Not me. And what about the cooking collection that now includes bottles of everything from rice vinegar to my husband's precious "Texas Pete" hot sauce? I wouldn't want to waste *those* beauties. And the batteries? We never leave 'em behind.

Enter the wonderful Ziploc freezer bag.

Boxing the cargo up without containing it could lead to some wonderful surprises when traveling across the country in a very hot car (the very reason movers won't pack them!), so I take precautions. When moving day approaches, I buy armloads of the more durable freezer Ziploc bags and put all small bottled liquids and anything that can melt into them.

Our method often works, but during our last move the plan failed us. It was June and my husband had returned from

Iraq the week prior to our move. With a newborn, a very inquisitive five-year-old, and the sale of our house pending, we were knee-deep in chaos.

The movers arrived on time to pack our goods and were unusually efficient, working quickly as the sun heated up our non air-conditioned house. My husband had diligently taped off a square on the floor where he put the items they were not to pack, another tactic that has worked well for us. The truck arrived the next day and away went all of our non-flammable, earthly possessions.

Per procedure, we packed the Hazmat Vehicle and drove off into the sunset, well, at least to the hotel down the road. The trip from New York to North Carolina was easier than most of our moves, so we made the entire drive the next day. Soon we pulled into our new home and began unloading the items we had transported. The moving truck arrived within the week and we set to unpacking boxes.

The relocation was deemed a success.

Until we couldn't find the cough syrup. And the Yankee Candles. And the bottles of shampoo I had bought on clearance to save a few bucks. The spare inhalers we had in case of a bad cold season. And what about the liquid soaps, shaving cream, bubble bath, hand creams, and dozens of other assorted containers? We sat down and reviewed the events of the move.

"Do you think the movers could have taken one of the boxes?" I asked my husband.

A hush fell over the room.

"Well," said my husband, "maybe they picked up one of the boxes when I was moving the stuff from the 'off-limits' area into the car. They probably put it on the truck without me realizing."

An unmarked box without a moving tag was as good as lost. And, as luck would have it, the box in question was full of all of the smallest and most expensive items in our liquids collection. With no word from the movers on our precious box, I finally had to admit defeat. No matter how skilled my husband was at manning the Hazmat Vehicle, or how good I was at the Art of Ziplocs, our battle plan had holes in it. We had failed to protect all of our hazardous items from the movers.

The mistake became a lesson learned, and it will not be repeated on our next move. My new plan involves locking up our "off-limits" items in one room and posting two tiny guards outside the door until the movers leave. A steady stream of M&M candies should keep the kids motivated during their duty. It's a solid plan, and I doubt anyone could make it through that front line!

JANINE BOLDRIN is the managing editor of *Military Spouse* magazine and former editor of *Military Kids' Life* magazine. She was an Army wife for 20 years. Janine lives with her three children in the Hudson Valley.

Grace
VALERIE H. ADAMS

On our first cross country move we met the most incredibly kind and generous people. My husband David's first assignment in the Air Force was at Wurtsmith AFB in Oscoda, Michigan. Since we were both from California, we really wanted to be assigned at a California base; however, there were very few stateside transfers available. We opted to "swap" with an airman who wanted to return to his home state of Michigan. A stateside swap meant we switched duty stations with someone who had the exact same rank and military specialty. It also meant that we had to foot the bill for the move. So we packed all of our personal belongings into a 1978 Chevy Blazer (we had rented a furnished apartment so we didn't have any large items) and set out for California in August of 1986.

At the time, my husband was an Airman First Class and I had held only part-time jobs so we had very little money. In fact, we had $500 cash and no credit cards. Needless to say, we were very anxious about the three-and-a-half day trip. Our first encounter with "kindness" was in Council Bluffs, Iowa. We had stopped at a shopping center to pick up a few necessities and found to our dismay that our car wouldn't start. As we sat there with the hood up, an older gentleman passing by asked if he could be of help. He actually diagnosed the problem—a broken fuel pump. Lucky for us there was a Napa Autoparts store in the shopping center. But, of course, we didn't have any tools to make the repair. The Napa clerk told us if we could wait a few minutes, he was getting off work and he'd be right out with the tools to fix it. Sure enough, some 30 minutes later he had us back in working condition and declined any payment for the service. Both men recognized that David was in the service and said it was their pleasure to help us out. These strangers have probably long forgotten their role in our lives, but we sure haven't! Thank you, Council Bluffs!

Our trip was uneventful until we reached Elko, Nevada. We pulled in to get gas and, to our utter horror, found that radiator fluid was spewing out the front of the grill. We asked the attendant if there was someplace open on a Sunday that could do the work. He said the regular stores were closed, but there was a guy who worked out of his garage who could do it. We drove through one of the older neighborhoods to find his shop and, sure enough, he was open for business. While he was mending the radiator, David and I debated the possibility that he would ask for a couple of hundred dollars for the repair. We steeled ourselves as he approached with the bill.

"That'll be $12.50," he said. I'm sure we didn't hide our surprised expressions at all. We were so grateful that we actually offered him $50! He declined, saying that he had served in Vietnam and he was more than happy to help a fellow serviceman.

Fortunately, the rest of the trip was without incident and we thoroughly enjoyed our subsequent five years at Castle AFB.

Since then we have been stationed in Iceland, Guam, San Antonio, Texas, and, most recently, Cheyenne, Wyoming. My husband retired in December 2007, and as I reflect back on all of our moves, I think most about our trip to California. The other moves have had their moments (kids add a whole new dimension to coordination, patience, and effort). But for that first move, we were vulnerable and practically penniless. Through the kindness of strangers we made it across the country.

VALERIE ADAMS and her husband David have two daughters. She is a scientist and spends her free time enjoying her family, horses, and Colorado.

The Pre-Move Adventure
LAURA ORNELAS

I'm sure this story will make us laugh in the years to come, but when it happened, it caused tears and blood pressure spikes. While living in New York, we got reassigned to Fort Hood, so we took an 11-day adventure to Texas to house hunt and then to New Mexico to attend our 20 year high school reunions. Everything seemed in order. We had our airline reservations, hotel reservations, rental car reservations, a tank full of gas, suitcases, money, everything. Little did we know what was in store for us.

Since we lived at Fort Drum, we (my husband Andrew and daughter Olivia) decided to fly out of Albany, New York, to save a thousand dollars on airline tickets. We drove over three hours to the airport and had plenty of time to check in and go through security. The airport was hot and crowded. Flights began getting canceled because of bad weather in New York City and Baltimore, so the waiting area got crowded. We noticed our flight number disappeared from the marquee above the gate, so I walked up to the counter to ask about it. Our flight was to take off at 5 p.m. and had been delayed until 7:45 p.m. We also found out it was 97 degrees outside and the air conditioning was broken in the airport. It was miserably hot with all those people in there! We sat and sat. Then they called us at 7:30 and said we could load, but we'd sit on the runway for an hour or two waiting to take off. That sounded like loads of fun. Off we went down the ramp. Of course, they couldn't sit my family together because that would have made sense. Apparently, that airline didn't do assigned seating, so we were scattered throughout the plane, each of us sitting among strangers who didn't want to give up a seat to have to sit in a middle seat. Who can blame them?

Our connecting flight in Newark was also delayed, ao again we sat in a tiny waiting area with 300 other tired and frustrated people. At the last minute there was a gate change, so we dashed up an escalator and across the terminal to get there. Once more we couldn't sit together. In fact, we were each given a middle seat.

Before getting on our plane, I called the hotel in Cedar Park, Texas, to tell them to hold our room as we'd be checking in late. Then I called the rental car company and asked them to hold our car and we'd pay for that day, but wouldn't pick up the car until they opened in the morning. The agent said, "No problem," and "Everything's taken care of." He told me they opened at 6 a.m. and he'd have it ready for me.

We landed at three in the morning and headed to baggage claim. Andrew's black bag: check. Olivia's green suitcase: check. My red suitcase? Where did it go? I went to the baggage claim office and discovered my luggage never left Newark. My contact lens solution, my glasses, every change of clothes, my toothbrush, toothpaste, and everyone's toiletries were in my bag. The airline gave me a tiny little "overnight kit" with a few things in it.

Nobody was around when we arrived at the rental car counter so we arranged ourselves on the nearby seating to catch a few hours of rest before the place opened. It's not easy to do with the stainless steel bars between each seat to prevent people from sleeping. Don't try napping at the Austin airport. That morning they tested the fire alarm system every three minutes. That went on for about an hour.

At 5:50 a.m., all the rental car companies began opening except ours. Finally some guy strolled in and turned on the light! I rushed to the counter and gave him my confirmation number and explained I had agreed to pay yesterday's fee and that Bill had held my car from the night before. Well, the new guy said there were no cars and that Bill had *not* done as he promised. They could upgrade me to a full size, he said, but would have to charge me the higher price, which was quite a bit more. I was exhausted from being up for 25 hours and frustrated from the delays, lost luggage, and the car company's inefficiency. I said I would not pay a higher rate because of their mistake! I was so mad. He said he could try to get some other agency to honor my price but he doubted they would.

The lady at the next counter said she would give us a compact car for our confirmed price. She redid the paperwork and said, "Sign here stating that you will not take the car out of Texas." We were going to a reunion in New Mexico! I started crying when she said she'd tear up the contract if we were taking the car out of state. The other counter agents also said they would not allow their cars to be taken out of Texas. So we said we'd park the car in El Paso and borrow my dad's car for the New Mexico leg of the trip, and that settled it.

We made it to the hotel in Cedar Park who had, in fact, held our room. Because of recent rains in Texas, the hotel was also known as "Cricket Central." We stepped over piles of crickets and killed the 40 or so that had invaded our room, and we got ready to meet with our realtor. We all showered and Andrew and Olivia got to change clothes. I, of course, had no suitcase.

Our realtor took us to look at four or five houses. We decided to make an offer on one. It was not the house of my dreams—it had a small yard and tiny bedrooms—but it was in good shape in a great neighborhood.

We gave the realtor all of the mortgage paperwork we'd secured before leaving New York. It wasn't what she needed, so we called our mortgage representative, who said he'd have it to us by the end of the day. Fantastic! My suitcase arrived just before bedtime, too!

Andrew picked a few crickets off his pillow and killed 30 more before we headed to bed. We put wet towels along the bottom of the door to keep them out of the hotel room.

Thursday morning we checked out of the hotel and headed for New Mexico. We snuck the car into Las Cruces, New Mexico, and parked it in my parents' garage where it safely stayed. On Friday morning, we borrowed my dad's Ford Escort and headed to Los Alamos for the reunion. As we pulled into Santa Fe, the realtor called and said she still hadn't gotten the correct paperwork. So we called the mortgage company and reminded him he had promised to have it to here by Wednesday night. It was now Friday afternoon! We stopped at an Office Max to send and receive some faxes. When we got back to the car we found that all four tires on the Escort had gone flat. We found an Alsups (New Mexico's version of 7-11) and re-filled them.

That evening we went to Sonic in Los Alamos for Slushees (Yum! No Sonics in New York!) before stopping at an old hangout called the Posse Shack for day one of my high school reunion. It was fantastic seeing everyone again, but before long, Andrew and Olivia had had enough of meeting people and listening to me catch up with old friends. As we left, I pulled the keychain out of my pocket and noticed the car key had broken! The plastic end you hold onto was there, but no long flat part that actually goes into the lock. Of course, a 1991 model car doesn't have remote openers. We searched the Posse Shack for that key with no luck. Then with a flashlight we looked inside the car and finally saw the piece on the floor, behind the locked doors. Anyone have a coat hanger?

Two or three friends went to work like car thieves for 30 minutes trying to break into the car. Nobody could get it open. I got another hanger and tried the other doors. Just when we thought all hope was lost, one of the door locks popped open. All those times I locked my keys in the car during high school paid off. It just took me a while to get the hang of it again.

The next day Andrew and Olivia headed for Belen, New Mexico, (just south of Albuquerque) for him to attend his reunion and for Olivia to spend some time with her cousins, Questen and Elise. Unfortunately, although they knew we were coming, Questen and Elise's parents decided to go camping instead, so when Andrew and Olivia showed up, nobody answered the door. Olivia ended up bunking with Grandma and Grandpa. She enjoyed that, but was disappointed about missing her cousins.

On Sunday morning Andrew picked me up in Los Alamos two and a half hours north of Belen, and we went to his reunion picnic Sunday afternoon after a short visit with his parents. We only stayed at the picnic for about an hour because it was so hot outside. Then we were off in the Escort for the long four-hour drive back to Las Cruces. The realtor called again while we were en route to report she still had not received the mortgage paperwork. When we got to Las Cruces, we stopped at Staples and faxed more documents to our lender, who promised his part would be done that night.

Monday morning we headed back to Cedar Park, Texas, in our rental car. We got the car across the state border like it had never left Texas! Unfortunately, at one point while going through road construction east of El Paso, a dump truck kicked up a rock which chipped the front window. We hadn't noticed until the crack started creeping up the windshield!

Somewhere east of Fort Stockton, (the halfway point between El Paso and Cedar Park) the realtor called to say she got the mortgage paperwork, but it wasn't what she needed. We called the mortgage broker again, who reassured us it was the correct information, and said he would call our realtor. By the time they resolved the paperwork issue, we lost the house to somebody else. The paperwork promised to us on Wednesday, was still not done by Monday afternoon causing us to lose that house!

The realtor also informed us she'd had a death in her family and had to leave town on Wednesday, so Tuesday was our last shot at finding a house that week, and there weren't many available in the school district we wanted. We finally arrived back in Cedar Park that evening.

We immediately called another mortgage broker and applied for a pre-approval.

We checked into another hotel, one that was cricket-free, and prepared to see some houses in the morning. The realtor showed us three houses, all small and with the same floor plan and horrible yards. The next house was fantastic—big, with a nice yard. We decided we wanted the big one, so I called the new mortgage broker, who had our paperwork in order and sent it to the realtor. Our bid went in at $10,000 under the asking price and was accepted! For the next few days we did some sight-seeing and got some much-needed rest. On Friday, we got the inspection done and asked that some simple things be fixed prior to closing.

We returned the rental car on Saturday with no punish-ment for the cracked windshield, checked our luggage, and got on our plane right on time! We flew to Atlanta, where we were delayed only 20 minutes, and then landed in Albany before dark. We retrieved all three suitcases. Things were definitely looking up. We were on the road home to be reunited with our 16-year-old son Zachary and our dogs and to sleep on air mattresses, since our household goods had been picked up weeks before.

We were two exits from home and the car died. It was about midnight by that time and pitch black on I-81. Luckily, we had some great neighbors who were still awake and rescued us. As suspected, the gas gauge had stopped working so a gallon of gas got us home.

After this misadventure, the actual move should be a piece of cake!

LAURA ORNELAS grew up in Los Alamos, New Mexico. She is a 1987 graduate of Los Alamos High School and earned a BA in Special Education from New Mexico Highlands University. She is married to LTC (RET) Andrew Ornelas. She was a Special Education teacher for 20 years and now is a professional dog trainer living in Midland, Michigan. The move to Michigan was her 14th (and last) move.

Moving Again and Again
CHRISTIE MORGANS

Part I: Moving Things

Here I go again. It's time to leave the house I've made into our home. Our precious things must be disassembled and the house sold. I began that process in the middle of the summer. Our lives went into a state of limbo and all artifacts and possessions were crammed into boxes. It should be so easy, this being our ninth, no tenth, move with the military. I have traveled from the South to the Southwest to the Midwest to the Northwest, then to the West, and now we're headed east to North Carolina, to see a new coast.

As much as I try to plan for this inevitable day, there is never enough time. I'm always caught still wearing pajamas when the moving truck rumbles up our driveway. I scurry frantically to place all sacred essentials into one allocated safe spot, the non-packing zone, usually on the kitchen floor. It's piled halfway to the ceiling—the suitcases, coolers, and trash bags full of linens, pillows and bedding. Safeguarding these vital textiles is the secret of evolved military wives, who know the sleeping bag saga when your belongings don't arrive at your destination the same time you do. My back certainly remembers those wonderful days of sleeping on the floor of our new place, before the moving department finally calls and says, "We have your things."

So I gather my composure, answer the door, and reluctantly let "them" in. Once the movers are in, my home is no longer mine. I am at their disposal and respond instantly to their yelled questions or else risk my precious possessions being packed haphazardly. I shuttle back and forth from room to room detailing my specifications, which the movers most certainly disregard the moment I leave. But I attempt some semblance of an organized plan. In my rookie years, the movers sensed my inexperience, and knew just how to handle me. They tossed around my things regardless of my requests. Broken items, lost memories, and tears resulted, until I realized I was in control, or had to at least pretend! Like poker players, we keep each other in sight now, no matter how long the day drags. Since we have more stuff now, this packing frenzy takes even longer. After twenty years of marriage and a teenage son, I have four glorious days to pack—and fall to pieces—and no place to relax.

Like many other moves, this one is painfully slow. I clean the house during the breaks. I don't realize how dirty we are until the beds and furniture are gone, so I scrub some more. For no reason, the garage door decides to go up and down. I assume it's malfunctioning, and add it to the list of things to fix. Later I discover the mover packed the opener in a box, and each time they stepped into the truck, the garage door opener activated.

Eventually, all items get tucked in their assigned boxes and stowed away. Day Four finally comes to a close, and we are officially done with the house. There is no evidence of our family here, except scattered nail holes in the walls and dust bunnies lying around. It is time to do a final wipe-down and say our goodbyes.

Part II: Moving Emotions

However physically grueling moving may be, nothing compares to detaching my emotions, cutting community ties, and preparing myself for another beginning. As a military spouse, I know I stepped into an adventure with the soldier I love. Deployments, training, travel, and moving are the conditions I live with, like it or not. I must adapt and overcome. With that said, I confess this last move was the most difficult one in my gypsy tale.

Each time I settled somewhere, I accepted that the friendships and memories were unique but temporary. I kept a healthy distance, so when I had to leave, I didn't miss those I knew so much. Those coping mechanisms got me through those goodbyes and hellos, but I often felt detached. I longed for a more solid foundation.

This house, in the sleepy little town of Chapman, Kansas, off the Great Plains in tornado alley, with all its crazy weather and beautiful sunsets, had been our home for three years. That wasn't much time to the average civilian, but it was enough for us to grow roots. Our family had flourished beyond what I anticipated. We felt settled and attached to the quirky little town of farmers, military families, and descendants of Irish immigrants. As reluctant as we had been to accept our new home, they too were less accepting of "newcomers." But by the time we had to leave that place, we had become a part of the community.

Our wonderful son, Matt, experienced each move with us and faced them all with courage and cool. He had attended ten different schools in his life. With much political wrangling, his father made sure he attended the same high school for three years prior to graduation. Matt had developed many friendships and excelled in academics and athletics, especially baseball. He'd also met the girl of his dreams many months earlier, and we were all amazed how much they had in common. They were inseparable. Never in my dreams could I have imagined how hard this move would be for us, but especially for him.

As scheduled, we left that home, cut the strings, and treasured the memories. Our son started college in North Carolina, tried to keep up his true love relationship from a long distance, but it ended in heartbreak. He regrets the move more than anything and remains in love with the girl he left behind.

I still feel loss from that last move. I finally found a place I called home, but with our lifestyle I couldn't hold on to it. It wasn't easy leaving and starting over again after I had truly felt like I found my home. But, deep down, I always know that home is where the Army sends us until our time of service is done. We are a military family, and like so many before us, keep moving again and again.

CHRISTIE MORGANS is a freelance artist, writer, and poet who was an Army wife for 21 years. They have one son. She lives in a lakeside home near Fort Bragg with her family and two dogs.

Strangers Packing My Underwear Drawer
SUZIE TROTTER

Even for a seasoned Navy wife who had survived five moves, including two overseas, in 12 years of service, the days leading up to packing day continued to be an anxiety-provoking time. This move was especially challenging while living in Naples, Italy, where my husband had just completed a three-year tour as the oral surgeon in the Dental Command. Although I had picked up some Italian during our travels, I still hadn't mastered the local dialect nor conversed fluently with anyone other than my language teacher. How was I going to communicate with these packers when they arrived? How could I be sure that they understood how each seemingly insignificant treasure my children created for me needed to be packaged as fragile goods? The kidney bean gingerbread ornament my daughter Sydney carefully crafted for me and the clay figurine resembling a blob my son Bradley molded with care had each survived the precarious move overseas and needed to get stateside with the same amount of protection.

Packing day arrived and, as usual, I was alone. My husband was out-processing and, thankfully, the children were at school. So I milled around, checking for last-minute things I should put in the suitcases we'd be living out of for the next two months. Then I heard the truck and my heart raced. This was it. There was part joy in knowing I'd be freed of the excess baggage, which meant no cleaning and no cooking. I often wondered why I had so much stuff as I enjoyed my moving "vacations" with all my worldly goods tucked away in containers. But I had to get through this day and tomorrow before I could begin to enjoy the next phase.

As the men—Renaldo, Giovanni, Eduardo, and Mimo—filed in, I calmed down; they looked familiar to me. I had not actually met *them* before, but men like them with their kind faces, joyful smiles, and animation. I didn't understand Italian very well, but it hadn't stopped me from getting my washer serviced, my gas tank filled, my door lock fixed, and other tasks accomplished during our tour, so I was comforted by their actions. They no longer felt like strangers to me. After our introductions and greetings, the team set into motion. With a lot of pointing, hand signals and short phrases, I directed the activities and gained some control of my personal space. Renaldo, the leader, asked me a few pertinent questions.

"Madame, no worry," he said. "We take care of everything." They immediately went to work and I awkwardly watched.

They had their own rhythm and methods. I tried to offer suggestions but kept receiving the same phrase: "No worry, Madame." I reached the point of reckoning that each military wife faces—the art of letting go and no longer being in charge. Although the active duty member had the written orders, the military spouse had the verbal power. Since I was usually the one with sole responsibility for household and children, it was difficult to shift into a lesser status. But I decided to accept my fate and try to enjoy it.

Since we were blessed to live in a flat above the best bakery in Naples, we woke up to the most amazing aromas and spoiled ourselves daily with fresh bread. I decided to show my appreciation to the packers in the way I do best: with a feast. The kitchen table was still accessible, so I filled it with fresh *mozzarella di bufola*, *proscuitto crudo*, ripe *melone* and warm rolls. Carefully placing the bottle of extra virgin olive oil we purchased from Tuscany among the platters, I offered communion to the men. We broke bread and forged a relationship where we were no longer strangers. Mimo spoke not a word of English, but he offered me his homemade sausage and spicy *friarelli* as a token of gratitude.

The next day continued as before, except this time I was among friends and enjoyed their silent company. I anxiously planned for the noonday meal and this time my husband joined us as the *barista* on the espresso machine. Mimo brought us some of his homemade wine and Eduardo offered me his portion of lunch.

"For you Madame. *Grazie.*"

"*Grazie* to you," I said in return, and wished I knew how to add, "Please take care of my meager belongings." But they knew.

At the end of the day, the very last thing that went into the crate was the kitchen table and chairs, the centerpiece of my relationship with these four men. It was bittersweet to see them go, but I was ready to move forward. Renaldo asked us to walk through the house to be sure they got everything. The cavernous and echoing flat came alive with the familiar, moving-day dust bunnies. Our walls were stripped of pictures, diplomas, and decorations, except for one item by the front door—the crucifix we bought in St. Peter's Square during the Millennium celebration. I carefully removed the cross, wrapped it in my "I Love Napoli" t-shirt and placed it in my suitcase. No strangers here. Just kindred spirits.

"*Grazie* my friends," I said to the four movers as they departed. "*Arrivederci.*" Fair winds and following seas.

Currently living on the Chesapeake Bay with her husband in Hampton, Virginia, SUZIE TROTTER enjoys all things water. She crews for women's sailing races, cruises with her husband on their sailboat, and volunteers on whale education boat tours for the Virginia Marine Science Museum and Aquarium. Their empty nest still fills with her daughter and son, along with family and friends who enjoy sharing in bayfront living. Follow her travel and foodie adventures on Instagram, @suzietrotter.

Normal, Or Something
Like It

My Kind of Normal
SONYA MOONEYHAM

The most common remark about military spouses I hear from civilians is: "I don't know how you do it." Well, I don't either! Very few of us are extraordinary. Mostly we're ordinary people doing what it takes to get through the day. Sometimes it's a matter of putting one foot in front of the other. We can reflect later. Sure, we often find ourselves in extraordinary situations. But while we are in the thick of it, we don't realize it.

Military life redefines "normal" for us. We can get used to anything and start to think it's the most normal situation in the world. Because, to us, it is. "Normal" is over-rated anyway. For better or worse, we make our own version of "normal."

As a Marine, my husband Sam is gone quite a bit, even when he's not deployed. We lived in Twenty-Nine Palms, California, for four years. During that time, Sam worked on the Fourth of July for the first three. On the fourth year, he was actually home and we were together. We had absolutely no idea what to do. My regular Independence Day was to spend it, well, *independently* from him. What were we supposed to do with him home all day on a holiday? That just wasn't normal.

Then there's moving. We sometimes prefer to call it PCS-ing. By now, I hope our friends and family have learned to record our address in pencil. It's guaranteed to change, sooner or later. We've moved across town, across the country, and around the world. There is nothing normal in the fact that we have provided our family and friends with eight different addresses in nine years. I didn't even realize it was that many until I took a moment to count.

My sister is not married to a military man. She has a difficult time when her husband is away for even a few days. She marvels at the apparent ease with which military spouses handle long absences and deployments. It isn't easy, but it's even harder with children. I complain all the time about being a "married single parent." Of course, complaining doesn't get the kids fed or to school on time or the baby's diaper changed. It's the nature of my husband's job that he isn't home for birthdays, anniversaries, holidays, and other milestones. That's just how it is. It's my job to keep things as normal as possible for the kids. We hold onto our routines of school, play dates, dinner, bath, and bedtimes. I'll admit to serving a lot more boxed pastas, frozen chicken nuggets, hot dogs, and anything else that can be microwaved or prepared in under 30 minutes. I do what I have to do.

Quite frankly, maintaining normal while Dad is gone is exhausting. Every day is the same: get up, send the kids to school, do laundry, write a letter or email to my husband, help with homework, make dinner, do bathtime, give goodnight hugs and kisses, go to bed, and do it all again tomorrow. It's tiring being the only parent available, staying upbeat in letters and emails, and acting like everything is fine. So I complain to other military spouses who are in the same boat. We commiserate a little before I get back to the business at hand: creating and maintaining our version of normal.

I had a friend who got so annoyed with her husband because he kept leaving shrapnel on her kitchen counter. (My husband informs me the correct term is "fragmentation.") It seems her husband was bringing home "trophies"—the metal that "just missed him" that day at the live fire range. I can see her point. If he wanted trophies of cheating death, fine, but leave them at the office. We don't want to know how close we came to widowhood, and we certainly don't want to be reminded of our husbands' dangerous lives over morning coffee. We need that time to convince ourselves that our lives are perfectly normal.

Most military spouses are doing the best they can to get through difficult circumstances. While we're trying to maintain normal, it's never far from our thoughts that our loved ones are far away from home in harm's way. Our children don't see their fathers for months at a time and the older ones know why. The parent left behind has to maintain the bond between the child and the absent parent and reassure both.

The reality is that for military children, having a parent gone for large chunks of their lives, even during the big milestones, is just another fact of life. It's not easy for them, but it's normal.

While I don't always recognize how extraordinary our circumstances are, I'm fortunate to have people in my life who remind me. I was telling a friend about how difficult our second child was to potty train. My friend pointed out that in the previous three months, my daughter had to deal with an international move, a new house and neighborhood, new daycare, and then Daddy deployed for a year. Oh, yeah. I guess I had my head down, putting one foot in front of the other, thinking everything was normal in my world.

SONYA MOONEYHAM was an Army brat and a lawyer before becoming a Marine wife. She and her husband have two daughters. They continue to live the nomadic life of a military family.

You Know You're a Military Wife When …
SARAH SMILEY

They were sitting beside me in the cement waiting room of a Navy branch clinic. They were talking to each other and smiling, so I knew they were newly married.

Now, I know what you're thinking: "Sarah, that's so stereotypical, jumping to conclusions and assuming that they are newly married simply because they were talking to each other and smiling. I mean, why didn't you assume something more obvious and reasonable, such as that they were boyfriend and girlfriend?"

Oh, well, that's easy. The young man, dressed in an olive green flight suit, couldn't have brought his girlfriend into the clinic to be seen. She wouldn't have had an ID card.

So, there I was reading a wrinkled and torn pamphlet about prostate cancer, while they held between them the ends of a brochure about their medical benefits. I was alone (Dustin was probably home with the kids or something), and they were huddled so close you'd have thought they were sitting in a teepee. I should also point out that the girl wore a fresh, coordinated outfit that not only looked clean, it looked ironed, too. I was wearing sneakers with no socks and a red baseball cap, because I don't get dressed up for a strep-throat culture.

Then the girl walked to the receptionist's desk to check on her appointment time.

"Last four?" the receptionist said.

The girl looked confused.

"Last four of your husband's Social," the woman said.

The girl turned around to her husband, still waiting in the chair, and said, "What's your Social Security number, honey?"

Right then, there was absolutely no mistaking—they were newlyweds. You can't be married to someone in the military for too long before you know their Social Security number like you know your own shoe size. In fact, I know my husband's "last four" better than I know my own.

All of which got me thinking. Just as there is a point at which a woman can no longer hide her pregnancy, there comes a time when a woman is undeniably a military wife. When does that happen? It's different for each person. Sometimes it even happens overnight, while you're unaware. Eventually, though, we all suffer the same fate. We wake up thinking, "When was the last time my mother wrote my address in ink in her address book?"

You might also realize you're a military wife when ...

· The site of US GOVERNMENT on your caller ID no longer freaks you out.

· All of your husband's fresh, white underwear has his "last four" stamped on the waist band.

· You know the smell of jet fuel.

· You laugh at *Top Gun*. Even harder at Tom Cruise as "Maverick."

· You know that APO isn't a type of dog food.

· Your husband's best friends have names like "GULA," "Wookie," "Rat Boy," and "Dancing Bear."

· Suddenly, "GULA," Wookie," "Rat Boy," and "Dancing Bear" seem like affectionate nicknames (although probably not to your civilian mother).

· You've had five different jobs in four years.

· You've had five different addresses in four years.

· You've had five new best friends in four years.

· Luckily, you've had the same husband for five years, but you haven't seen him in three.

· You know that "Haze grey and underway" is not a song by Neil Young.

· When your husband announces he's going to use "the head," you no longer smirk and think, "About time... but I'm still smarter than you."

· You realize that when your husband is on "cruise," he

won't be dining with the captain of the *Love Boat*.

· Similarly, you realize your junior husband won't be dining with any captain.

· You know that your husband will eat in the Mess Hall, and you think that's right where he belongs.

And last, you definitely know you're a military wife when you're sitting in a waiting room without your husband and you're not the least bit jealous of the girl who doesn't know her husband's "last four." (Even if she was thinner and had better skin.) Because you know, without a doubt, that she's got a lot to learn and a long way to go.

Navy wife SARAH SMILEY is the author of a syndicated newspaper column and four memoirs: *Got Here as Soon as I Could, Dinner with the Smileys, I'm Just Saying,* and *Going Overboard.* She's best known for writing about motherhood (she has three sons) and life in the military. Over the years, she has also received attention for her columns about depression, politics (particularly regarding the military and motherhood), baseball, and life in Maine. In 2014, Sarah was awarded the American Legion Auxiliary's prestigious national Public Spirit Award. Find out more at www.sarahsmiley.com.

The Greatest Good
RUTHIE ALEKSEYEV

The best military spouse movie scene ever is not even about military spouses! Have you seen it? If you have kids, you'll know exactly which movie I'm giving the dialogue from. You can probably even recite the lines along with me:

Frozone: Honey, where is my super-suit?
Honey: What?
Frozone: WHERE IS MY SUPER-SUIT?!
Honey: Uh, I put it away.
Frozone: Where?
Honey: Why?
Frozone: I need it!
Honey: WHY do you need to know?
Frozone: I need it!
Honey: Uh-uh! Don't you think about running off doing no derrin'-do. We've been planning this dinner for two months!
Frozone: The public is in danger!
Honey: My evening is in danger!
Frozone: You tell me where my suit is, woman! We are talking about the greater good!
Honey: Greater Good? GREATER GOOD? I am your WIFE! I am the greatest GOOD you are EVER going to get!

Since Frozone shows up later in the movie (*The Incredibles*, for those who haven't guessed yet) in full regalia with his blue super-suit and identity-hiding mask to save the world, we can only assume his wife dealt with her feelings and gave him the super-suit so he could go do his job and save the world. I can totally relate.

I can't count the number of plans that my husband Jacob, an OSI (Office of Special Investigations) Agent in the Air Force, and I have had to scrap because the urgent call came down the chain of command for him to stop what he was doing, put on his super-suit, and go save the world from one imminent threat or another. Or at least to take some class learning how to save the world from an imminent threat. It's not always deployments—TDYs both short and long take a toll, too.

For example, there was the time three days before our anniversary when he had less than 24 hours to get on the only plane available to fly into Greenland. I was not graceful in my acceptance of the inevitable. I'm sure there are still mountains ringing with the echoes of my less-than-polite language.

But I still do it. I cancel the dinner reservations and dig out the super-suit, sometimes grudgingly and other times in a breathless whirlwind of trying to help. In anticipation of a possible Air Force-sponsored change in plans, I always buy the more expensive travel tickets that can be rescheduled, and I seem somewhat flaky to many of my civilian friends and family members because we've had to bow out of so many planned activities.

I know now, after a long time as a military spouse, that I married a man who isn't "normal" and run-of-the-mill. I didn't just marry him; I married his super-suit too. And because his super-suit is so much a part of who he is, I have to love it and all the baggage that comes with it.

That doesn't mean I run around wearing red, white, and blue and singing the national anthem 24 hours a day. Sometimes I get very angry about our lack of stability and seeming inability to have a "normal" family vacation. Or a "normal" anniversary together. Or my husband home when my children learn to walk or have some other milestone. Sometimes I feel a lot of despair. Sometimes I want to buy my own private island and set up a tin pot dictatorship that doesn't involve deployments and TDY.

But somehow I think that even if Jacob and I had our own country (with me as Commander-in-Chief, of course), complete with tax code and seat in the UN General Assembly, Jacob would form an alliance with some other country that would require him to put on his super-suit and rush off to save the world on a moment's notice. That's just who he is.

And me? I understand him, and I run our family accordingly. That makes me the greatest good he's ever going to get.

RUTHIE ALEKSEYEV has been a National Guard wife, an Air Force wife, and a writer for Spousebuzz.com. She and her husband have four children and live in Florida.

Live It, Breathe It, Blow It Up
RENÉ LOWE

Toy planes rumble and whoosh through the air. They maneuver and scuffle, with fingers lofting each aircraft higher and higher. Bodies lean left and hands propel fighter jets through the clouds. My eyes blur. I shake the fog from my temples.

No, that's not my friend's son. It's my husband. I'm not in a backyard with a bunch of little boys. I'm at the Naval Air Station Oceana Officers' Club or O'Club for short. I look back at my fly guy and roll my eyes. There he is again, bobbing and weaving, reconstructing his earlier flight. He stops to gulp his beer, parched from talking too much, one hand still high in the air. He's pulling Gs, his right-handed F-18 Super Hornet coming from underneath the left-handed Russian MiG-29, twisting and evading each other. The MiG is trying to avoid being shot down by his 20 mm Gatling gun. My wanna-be first grader says something like, "There I was, reaching the attack window, executing a max performance turn. I arrived in his control zone and saddled in for a guns kill. Then I said to my adversary, 'Knock-it-off' and 'Let's set up another engagement.'"

My husband shakes out his hands, tired from a grueling hour of sign language flights. He picks up his beer, nonchalantly now, as if his little dance didn't happen.

Every Wednesday and Friday at the Oceana O'Club, a sea of olive green flight suits congregate to conduct their airborne symphonies. The O'Club was legendary in its day. The boys got together to shake off the work week with a drink, tell a few stories, and talk about flying.

There's always a deployment video with night vision footage from infrared weapons systems and panoramic views from the cockpit on one of the many televisions in the bar. I've seen my guy talk about weekend plans until he catches a glimpse on the screen of someone shooting missiles or dropping bombs and off he goes talking about deployment shenanigans and flying again.

Oceana O'Club is decorated with vertical tails of old aircraft, flight gear displays, and Navy plaques and awards. It's one giant "Love-Me Wall" the guys can only dream of having. Most wives I know dutifully find a small, discreet place to hang all the plaques, awards, and fighter jet pictures from their husband's work. But the Brits do it right. The British Marines display their love-me walls in their bathrooms, a compact space where a guy can go to reminisce about the glory days.

I really can't blame my fly guy for never growing up. Tactical aircraft (TACAIR) flyers have replica planes-on-a-stick at the squadron to demonstrate techniques with one another. These grown men brief and debrief after each flight, playing with their models to reconstruct what happened. So, playing at the O'Club is just an extension of training, right?

But it gets worse.

For practice, the Navy has my guy strap some bombs onto his jet, fly to the desert and blow scrap metal to bits for a living. So why, when he drops ordnance on a defenseless 1972 Pinto at the weapons range all day, does he need to come home, sit in front of the computer, and play video games?

Sports games, flying games, shooting games—he never tires of conquering new worlds. I don't understand how he can sit there for hours going through the same scenarios, gunning and firing over and over again. Sure, he gets to shoot the enemy with cool virtual weapons, but when does he unplug himself and help with the dishes?

Between the hand flying, stick planes, and video games, my guy can be one of the boys forever. No need to grow up when these behaviors are reinforced and encouraged by all the other aviators he plays with day in and day out.

So will my husband and his comrades ever grow up? Not in this life as long as they can live it, breathe it, and blow it up.

RENÉ LOWE is an Information Technology Project Manager working in Health IT. Her experience as a former Army Medical Service Corps officer and the former spouse of a Naval Aviator gives her a unique insight into military life.

The DITY Gazebo
LEE ANNE GALLAWAY-MITCHELL

My husband Brad found the gazebo for 50-percent off at Wal-Mart. It was a 10-by-10, four-cornered, steel structure topped with a double-tiered, pagoda-style roof of beige canvas. The picture on the slim rectangular box featured the structure sitting on a neatly manicured lawn at dusk, mosquito netting curtains loosely tied to each of the four cast-iron, corner posts. The River Delta Canopy gazebo glowed with sophistication and romance.

Brad kept these 100 pounds of "Easy Assembly" wedged behind a shelf of grilling tools and gardening supplies where it awaited summer. When I arrived at our home as a new bride, the gazebo remained out of sight. He never kept its existence a secret. Brad was proud of his purchase. But when summer arrived, we realized we had nowhere to put it. The backyard sloped about 45 degrees.

A month before my husband deployed to Afghanistan, we decided to move on base where a home was miraculously available. Since it was the busy moving month of August, we could not arrange movers through the military, so we moved ourselves. Known as a Do-It-Yourself or "DITY" Move, this program pays about 95% of the government's cost directly to families, who take care of their own packing and moving.

Within a week, we had packed and vacated the other house. Between cleaning and packing and moving everything across town, we neglected to mow our grass on base. We received our first yard ticket in what must have been record time. Every week a little tan truck drove up and down the streets of base housing looking for tall grass, sloppy edging, and cluttered carports. Offenders found tickets on their doors detailing the offense with a tally of demerits. Of the 15 points allowed before facing eviction, we earned 12 the first week. We put off unpacking for yard work.

The boxes remained unpacked for another week while I

attended orientation for my new job and Brad prepared for deployment. We had two weeks before he left, and I wanted to spend at least one free weekend settling in and assembling our bed. On Saturday, I started the slow work of unpacking and putting stuff away. By Sunday, the mattress still sat on the floor along with boxes that Brad had yet to organize, many of which had not been unpacked through several moves. Different colored inventory tags covered them like luggage labels. I started looking for Brad and found him outside.

The banged-up box containing the gazebo had made the move. After seeing it leaning against the small storage shed, Brad decided to assemble it in our large, flat backyard. With the contents spread out on the concrete patio, he sat in the August heat, fighting mosquitoes and poorly written instructions. It looked like a two-person job, one that would take me away from my unpacking. However, if I helped, the sooner the damn thing would be up and the sooner he would help me unpack. I stepped outside and he immediately put me to work. I held the corners together as he fastened them with screws. As soon as the frame was standing, I got to work on the roof while he tightened the dozens of screws holding together the frame.

The roof was not easy; the materials were cheaply made and fit poorly. Since the roof had two tiers, I had to assemble each one separately, then fit the smaller roof into the settings welded onto the larger one. As soon as I got one beam into place, another would shift and throw off the balance. The mosquitoes were as merciless as the sun; I wanted to go back inside. We had been sleeping on the floor for over a week and our bed beckoned. Near tears, I wondered why the gazebo was suddenly such a priority.

"Why are we doing this?" I asked, attempting to hide a beam I had just broken.

My husband looked at me. "I don't want it to rust and go to waste. Besides, you need somewhere to read and grade papers."

Brad went back to work, and he was taking his sweet time about it, too. He pondered the task before him, took an occasional sip of beer, and resumed work.

I went inside while Brad stayed and finished the job, almost. He completed the frame and assembled the roof. The canvas covering the roof stretched past its limit and tore in places. The roof, though lopsided, would probably look fine once in place. But it stayed right where it was—sitting in the grass like a deformed camping tent.

One week later, the roof remained in the middle of the backyard. Brad was leaving in a week, and the gazebo had been abandoned over the piles on the floor: t-shirts, flight suits, socks, boxers, and everything else he needed to take to war.

"Don't worry; we'll have people over for drinks and steaks. We'll have a roof-raising," he said.

We had the drinks and the steaks and the people, but the roof stayed on the ground. The rest of the structure stood complete yet roofless beside our patio. After Brad left, I pondered what to do with the roof. For the rest of that fall, I mowed around it and lived in fear of the little tan truck that patrolled the yards on Tuesdays. By November, the canvas sagged beneath the weight of pine needles. It was time for the roof to go. Feeling guilty, I collected all the pieces in a box and mowed the yellowed grass underneath.

My husband came home in January. We said little about the gazebo. April came, and we started a vegetable and herb garden. The four corners of the roofless gazebo made perfect climbing trellises for my tomatoes. Brad strung up Christmas lights, weaving them among the scrollwork. In May, he put canvas over the top of the frame to protect us from the sun and added misters, garden hose-like tubing that sprayed cool water.

It is August, almost a year to the day when he started building the gazebo, only to leave it in pieces on the lawn. We now have a lovely garden sheltered by a sturdy cast-iron frame. Lights sparkle at night, and the misters give us relief from the heat as we sit in the gazebo and drink our wine. We never needed that flimsy roof.

What I failed to realize a year ago, but what I do know now

after one deployment and a year of marriage, is that building the gazebo calmed him. For a couple of hours that afternoon, he was not leaving me. He was just in the moment, one of sublime ordinariness, when the biting mosquitoes and the North Carolina heat were the only things he had to fight.

Just when we have our garden and our shelter from the sun, we have to move again. Our gazebo will not make the trip. My husband will find other things to build, projects that will be interrupted by training and deployments. But I will not fret over those unfinished pieces. They will be waiting for him when he returns.

LEE ANNE GALLAWAY-MITCHELL earned a PhD in English from the University of Texas and now writes and teaches in Tucson where she lives with her husband and their two children. She is an MFA candidate in creative writing at the University of Arizona. Her work has been published in *Iron Horse Literary Review, O-Dark-Thirty, Chagrin River Review,* and *Sun Star Lit.*

Keeping it Together
(Barely)

Pickles and the U.S. Navy
DESIREÉ COLVIN

When I was first engaged to my husband, I had a conversation with my mother about what it would be like to be a Navy wife. I believed I was pretty well-informed about what I was getting into, but couldn't possibly know everything. Personally experiencing things was going to be different than reading about them.

"Nobody can guess the future," my mom said quietly, "but I'm sure you'll do fine in this new life."

"What makes you so sure?" I asked.

"You've always been the most independent of my three girls," she said. "In fact, your favorite phrase was always, 'Mother please! I can do it myself!'"

And that is just the phrase that came to mind after my husband left on a detachment to the Middle East.

Ten months after our wedding day and one week after he left, I was in the kitchen cleaning up, putting away groceries and congratulating myself on how well I'd done that week. Sure, I missed my husband, but I was doing okay. I'd traveled across the country alone to my sister's wedding. I had changed the oil in the car and had plans to work on the transmission. I was doing fabulously with the finances and had already put extra into savings. Here I was, on my own and doing fine. "I can do this!" I told myself. "It's hard but, by golly, I can do this!"

After all the groceries were put away, I decided it was time for a little snack. I pulled out a jar of pickled okra. (Since I'm from San Antonio, Texas, okra is a staple in my diet and a comfort food. I once grew okra in my mother's garden as a kid and won first place with it at the county fair!) I tried opening the jar. No luck. I tried again. It wasn't budging. Third time's the charm? No. I grabbed a tea towel and used it to get traction. There was less traction than before. "This cannot be happening," I thought. "I can change the car oil and I can't open a jar of pickles?"

The situation quickly grew desperate. This okra had suddenly become much more than a snack. It was a metaphor for this entire separation from my husband. If I couldn't handle a vacuum-sealed jar of okra, then how on earth was I supposed to handle the next couple of months? Our next door neighbor, a strong fellow who flew helicopters for the Navy, was at work. The neighbor on the other side was also on detachment. There was nobody. It was me against the pickles and there wasn't a man in sight to come to my rescue.

I put all of my unimpressive 113 pounds into the task, holding back the tears as I began to think I wouldn't have pickles for months until my husband came home and opened the jar for me. That was simply unacceptable. I wanted, I *needed*, these pickles. I had to prove I could do this, that I was capable. I ran the jar under warm water. I banged the lid on the counter top. I gave it one last desperate twist, and to my utter surprise and amazement, I heard the very satisfying "pop" as the vacuum seal broke. Success! I had done it. I had really, truly done it, but not without the realization that perhaps I wasn't quite as independent as I (or my mother) thought.

As I savored the first bite of that fantastic, and duly earned, okra pickle, I cried. I cried so much that even I didn't know I owned that many tears. They were an odd mixture of joy and sadness. I knew I was going to make it through the rest of this detachment come hell, high water, or vacuum-sealed jars. I also knew I missed my husband desperately. While being extremely proud of him and what he does for this great country and equally proud of myself and my ability to handle the daily tasks of life, I realized in that okra-pickle-jar moment just how much I loved and needed my husband.

DESIREÉ COLVIN, a Navy wife, is a violinist and music teacher. She enjoys traveling, scrapbooking, and reading anything by or about Jane Austen.

Taxing the Wife
MARTHA MERRITT

Every military wife is accustomed to being disoriented. Any PCS move would be easier if we had our own personal escort to help us navigate the unfamiliar territory we are forced to tackle with each new location. But every military wife is also accustomed to pushing through the discomfort of disorientation and handling those responsibilities that we pride ourselves on accomplishing while our soldiers aren't around.

Disorientation set in the first day my husband and I moved to Kansas. Since housing wasn't available at the time of our move to Fort Riley, my husband and I found a house in a town fifteen miles from post. Our house was beautiful and the city was friendly, but living off-post left me clueless when it came to navigating Fort Riley. New to the military life, and intimidated by my lack of knowledge regarding on-post etiquette, I hadn't even made a trip to the commissary. Just weeks after our move, and dangerously close to April 15, I had to venture on post to find Tax Services.

My husband gave me directions the night before. This is where I should interject that my husband is one of the most directionally-challenged people I know. He often got confused giving directions, and yet he made it sound like finding the Tax Center would be a cinch. His directions seemed simple enough, and I left the house the next morning feeling confident that I knew where I was going. Right.

I drove on post feeling optimistic at first. I remembered these roads from the two brief times I'd been there, and I accurately predicted what road came next. I had the hang of this! I will admit, though, that Fort Riley can be pretty intimidating; I've never seen so many one-way roads and traffic circles in my life! I continued cruising along, knowing that the way I chose was technically the long way, but the least confusing for a newcomer. I didn't mind because the weather was beautiful, and I enjoy driving with the windows down.

Eventually, I realized that I must have passed the Tax Center. I found myself on the road that ran parallel to where I was supposed to be. However, there were no crossroads to get me there. I could *see* the road, but could not *get* there. Tax Services was tucked away on a little one-way street that was impossible to find or get to because I had to drive around somewhat aimlessly through one traffic circle after another. It became like that scene in *National Lampoon's European Vacation*, "Hey, look kids! Big Ben! Parliament!" I drove those traffic circles a hundred times!

Frustrated, I decided to consult the "map" my husband drew for me on yellow sticky notes the night before. I pulled into a parking lot, took out the map, and looked at random arrows, scribblings with no street names, and no indication of which way was north. It was useless.

I drove in circles for another half an hour while the April temperature crept up. I continued my aimless wandering as impatient soldiers tailgated me, and my car quickly became an Easy Bake oven. With blood pressure rising, I called my husband at work and asked him how in the world to get to where I needed to be.

He asked where I was. "The PX," I said. "Help!"

"Hmmm...hmmm...I'm not sure," he replied. I felt even more frustrated, and since I was parked in one place (no talking on the cell phone while driving on post), the sun had started to fry my leg, and I was quite sure I'd need a skin graft to get the denim off my thigh.

I told him I'd figure it out myself, even though I had no clue how I would. I had already tried that plan, and where did it get me?

For a while, I just picked a random car and followed it. It was April; maybe they were going to the Tax Center, too. Needless to say, I gave up on that plan rather quickly. After 45 minutes of driving around, getting baked, and becoming increasingly cranky, I somehow found the magic road which took me to the elusive one-way that led to Tax Services. I'm sure that God took pity on me and moved that road directly in front of my car because, I *swear,* I had been that way a million times!

I made it to Tax Services only to find out that—wouldn't you know it—they needed another signature from my husband on the final forms. Tax forms in hand, I sped off post, leaving Fort Riley in a cloud of dust. But not before making another wrong turn and meeting, yet again, two more traffic circles.

MARTHA MERRITT is a proud Army wife who lives with her husband, Clinton, near Fort Riley, Kansas. She teaches high school English and enjoys writing in her free time.

Sickest Child

SARAH SMILEY

My mom always says, "Mothers are only as happy as their saddest child." I don't know if she coined the phrase or heard it somewhere else, but whenever I'm feeling down because one of my boys (Ford, Owen, and Lindell) is sick, discouraged, or otherwise having a hard time, I think of Mom and know that she was right. I will never be any happier than my saddest child.

For the last six weeks, everyone in my family has taken turns being sick. Back-to-back illnesses have invaded our home. During a four-week stretch my boys alternated being home from school. I was beginning to feel claustrophobic stuck inside the house, and my husband, Dustin, just couldn't understand why. He of course still went to work every day and even made a trip—for "flight-training purposes"—to Key West.

It all started back in October, when Owen, then 3, had a blocked intestine (hope you aren't eating) which resolved just in time for his already scheduled tonsil- and adenoidectomy. The next two weeks were a blur. As Owen slowly recovered, Dustin, home for a few hours each night, made comments like, "Wow, it's emotionally draining when they're sick, isn't it?" This kind of reminded me of how he once said that the "most tired" he's ever been was when I was in labor.

Owen rallied in time for Thanksgiving, and our lives were getting back to normal, if only for 24 hours. Then Ford got pneumonia. Twice.

It was around this time that Dustin made his trip to Key West for training. When he called from a noisy street corner to tell me about the great restaurants and bars, I couldn't wait to tell him about all the "excitement" here at home: I had folded five loads of laundry, Ford had a fever, and Owen went to the bathroom on the floor, not once, but three times.

Yes, I was angry that Dustin wasn't home to help. I even

yelled at him over the phone, reminding him of all the times he's been gone—on deployment or on "training missions" to the most sought-after vacation destinations—just when we need him most.

All Dustin said was, "I promise, I wish I were there."

He would rather be home with sick kids than whooping it up in Key West?

I didn't believe him.

Yet as my anger wore off I realized that as bad as it had been the past six weeks, there's no place else I would have rather been than at home with Ford and Owen. I couldn't imagine being in Key West or Paris or even Hawaii when one of my children is sick and needs me.

Our service member spouses miss a lot while they are gone, and sometimes it seems unfair that they miss more than their share of nights spent awake with a sick child and harried trips to the emergency room. In our desperation, we might actually believe our spouses rejoice in what seems like deliberately shirked responsibilities. But the truth is, we have become so focused on their absences at Christmas, birthdays and other happy occasions, we forget that perhaps the hardest time to be away from home is when your family needs you. If we think missing Thanksgiving is tough, imagine being halfway across the world while your son is in the hospital. My guess is that many service members would trade all the missed anniversaries and birthdays just to be home every time their child was sick or their spouse was crying on the living room floor.

On the phone I acted as if Dustin was purposefully missing-in-action when we needed him. What he tried to tell me, but I couldn't hear, was that as beautiful and fun as Key West may be, it's nothing compared to being home with your family to help them through the bad times. He wasn't celebrating the fact that he dodged the midnight shift with a feverish Ford. Instead he was trying to get home as soon as possible.

Because even when you're on vacation—oops, excuse me, *when you're on a training mission*—in a sunny place like south Florida, you're still only as happy as your saddest child.

Navy wife SARAH SMILEY is the author of a syndicated newspaper column and four memoirs: *Got Here as Soon as I Could, Dinner with the Smileys, I'm Just Saying*, and *Going Overboard*. She's best known for writing about motherhood (she has three sons) and life in the military. Over the years, she has also received attention for her columns about depression, politics (particularly regarding the military and motherhood), baseball, and life in Maine. In 2014, Sarah was awarded the American Legion Auxiliary's prestigious national Public Spirit Award.

The Easy Life
SUZIE TROTTER

I began my nursing career in 1986 in the Special Care Nursery at Indiana University Medical Center. While working the night shift saving lives, I subsisted on adrenaline, Cheerios, and Diet Pepsi. I loved it. I was full of energy and professionally fulfilled. Before long, I married my high school crush, Brad, a second-year dental student, and we looked forward to establishing ourselves in our hometown of Indianapolis. As graduation loomed, claustrophobia overcame us. We knew that starting a dental practice would be confining. The burden of owning a business combined with call hours would be all-consuming, and we felt trapped and panicked. We still had a burning desire to explore and learn about each other in our new relationship before settling in for a permanent residence with little opportunity to travel. That's when the Navy came into the picture. Brad came home early in the spring before graduation and said he'd spoken to the Navy recruiter at school. He shared the options with me and we agreed that a three year commitment was not only reasonable but exciting and just the thing we were searching for before settling in. Upon graduating, he received his lieutenant commission, and we excitedly anticipated our first tour of duty.

We moved to Parris Island, South Carolina, with a three-month old baby. Seeing my handsome husband in his summer whites surrounded by the beauty and pageantry of the Marines was a dream come true. The Blue Angels flew over my house routinely and we enjoyed an abundance of fresh shrimp, as much as we could net during high tide. Life in the Low Country was easy. Until the first bounced check! With the increased cost of uniforms and the miniscule lieutenant's pay, our disposable income had dramatically decreased! It was clear I needed to return to work in order for us to stay afloat financially.

I began working in the nursery at the local hospital, trying to balance daycare costs with meager pay. As an experienced nurse, I had no difficulty finding employment; this was the case through our next three moves and seven more years of service. The Dental Corps was good to my husband and we enjoyed the adventure. Then an unbelievable opportunity presented itself. My husband finished his oral surgery residency at Portsmouth Naval Hospital and received orders to the Naval Hospital in Naples. We were off to Italy!

We decided it was time for me to be the "stay-at-home mom" I craved. It was my turn for the easy life. But it didn't take me long to realize that the dream I had did not match the reality in this foreign country.

We experienced frequent car trouble, but thankfully there was a garage on base that provided service. We owned a 1986 BMW, which was nothing special as everyone in Naples had an old, dented BMW. We replaced the clutch, front wheel bearings, starter, front right axle thingy, windshield, cracked tires, plus a few other random things. Sergio, the mechanic, became my friend through my frequent garage visits. One evening, my husband called me from outside our house to help him push the stalled car out of the garage. This can't be good, I thought to myself. The next morning he gave me a peck on the cheek with the parting words, "Call and get the car towed and I'll see you later." My eloquent response wasn't nearly as cheerful. At that point, I wanted to trade in my easy life for double shifts of intense hospital work.

I continued with my morning routine as I figured stress could wait until I fixed another cappuccino. Then I placed a call to my friend Vicenzo, the tow truck guy referred to me by Sergio.

"*Buon giorno, Signore!*" All formalities aside, he wanted to know where I was. I explained I was at my home in Monteruscello. Fine, he said, he'd come. I informed him the car was below in the garage, not on the street.

"Oh," he said. "I cannot come. I cannot find you."

"Yes, yes, Vicenzo. You've been here before!" I pleaded. I explained I was easy to find as I lived above the *panetteria*, the bakery. He agreed to call me when he was in the area in about 20 minutes.

"What is your phone number?" he asked.

"524-2595," I replied.

"5429?"

"No," and I repeated it.

"9525?"

"No. 2595"

"Is that 529?"

I repeated it one last time.

"Va bene," he said, and hung up. Now, I knew full well he didn't have my phone number!

So I positioned myself on the balcony to watch for him. When I saw him drive by my house without slowing down, I called him again.

"Vicenzo, I think you passed me."

"No, *Signora,* your street is too small. I cannot come," he replied. Somehow I got him to agree to try. This time I stood in the street and waved him down, which prompted a barrage of honking horns, blowing kisses, and google-eyes, otherwise known as flattery gone sour!

My landlord, Mario, and his wife observed the circus from the garage, where they were unloading their freshly-grown produce from his car. Vicenzo backed down to the garage to hook the BMW to his tattered tow rope. His truck bed was longer than the short driveway which had a 45 degree angle leading down into the garage. As he descended, the truck bed screamed and dug into the cement, gravel scattering, and the right tail-light popped out of his tow truck! Mario scratched his head and his wife blurted, *"Mama mia!"* as she sat primly snapping beans for market.

As we repeated the scene going up the driveway, the left tail-light popped out of Vicenzo's truck and I ran over it with the BMW. Again, Mario's wife grimaced, *"Mama mia!"* I apologized to Vincenzo, *"Mi dispiace."* Scratching his head in bewilderment he replied, "Me, too!"

Once we got the car out of the garage and ready to take to the shop, Vicenzo opened the door for me to climb in the cab of his truck. Good thing I was wearing black shorts as the inside was dirtier than the bottom of my shoes after a day at the track.

"You want a smoke?" Vicenzo offered. Even though I didn't smoke, at that point I even considered it! Little did I know the adventure was just beginning. The bumpy ride to base made me feel like a Jell-O Jiggler. As we got close to our exit, there were new vibrations when a tire on his truck blew! Cute little Vicenzo smiled and said, "It's no problem. We go get it fixed." We wobbled down the *autostrade* with a blown tire that sounded like we were being chased by a mummy with a steel coffin on one foot. Now my flab had taken a new direction, and I had an angular pitch as if you hit the side of a table holding Jell-O Jigglers.

Outside his friend's shop, Vicenzo parked his truck facing the *oncoming* traffic. Cars blazed past me. Then I heard noises: *jerk, jerk, clink, clink*, and a big *clink*. As the jack lifted the truck with me in it, my flab resting solidly on my right hip, I wanted to shout, "Hey, Vicenzo, got a cigarette?" Fifteen minutes later with the tire fixed, we rolled into the garage on base.

Sergio the mechanic saw me and extended his arms with a warm embrace. "Mrs. Trotter, what's the matter this time?" Exhausted, I explained.

"No worry," he said. I told him maybe I should get a job at his shop since I was there quite often. Come to think of it, a job sounded really good about then. I wanted to trade in my "easy life" for one with a little less stress!

Currently living on the Chesapeake Bay with her husband in Hampton, Virginia, SUZIE TROTTER enjoys all things water. She crews for women's sailing races, cruises with her husband on their sailboat, and volunteers on whale education boat tours for the Virginia Marine Science Museum and Aquarium. Their empty nest still fills with her daughter and son, along with family and friends who enjoy sharing in bayfront living. Follow her travel and foodie adventures on Instagram, @suzietrotter.

A Funny Thing Happened
on the Way

A Change of Life
BETTY PACKARD

I came into this Army life a little later than most. After 15 years of widowhood, I was introduced to an Army Recruiting Commander at a party, and I like to say that he made the most important recruit of his life that night. Soon after our marriage, the Army transferred him to Command Headquarters in Indianapolis where I lived. In the beginning, things weren't too different except that he left the house before daylight at an hour he called "oh-dark-thirty" and went to bed fairly early at night. For this night owl, that took a little adjusting.

When the Army said he had to go to Korea on a one year unaccompanied tour, I sent him off with nary a whimper. After all, I had maintained a household and raised two children into mid-teenage years by myself; I was quite confident a year apart wasn't going to cause any problems.

But then one day he called from Korea to tell me that we were moving. Moving? I hadn't thought about that as being part of this marriage equation. I had lived in the same home for 18 years and friends suspected it would take dynamite to get me out of the area.

"Why are we moving?" I asked.

"Because the Army said so," he replied.

I thought about that for a while. "You'll love it," he said with some forced joviality. When I asked him where we were going, he told me Fort Ord.

"Wow!" I commented sarcastically. "And where, pray tell, is that?" My shock was tempered when he told me that it was in Monterey, California, my favorite vacation spot in the world. And so Steve came home from Korea and I set about packing up the house while he dealt with something called "Transportation."

We decided to drive out together. It would acquaint me with Fort Ord, and then I would fly back and move us once a house became available. Now, *my* idea of driving is stopping to see all the marvelous scenes along the way. Steve's idea is to get from Point A to Point B without stopping once. But since he was still unsure of how I was going to take this move, he bit his tongue and stopped more times than he has ever done since.

We arrived at Fort Ord about a day later than Steve had mentally planned. He went into the housing office, came out with a key and we were ushered into something called "Visiting Officers Quarters." It was a drab and sterile place. One look at my face and Steve cheerfully announced that we should immediately go for a drive and check out this great new place called Monterey. We were soon winding our way down the peninsula, enjoying the beach and what I thought was the ocean but learned later was Monterey Bay.

We saw a sign that said "17-Mile Drive" and decided that's where we should go. The gate guard asked if we were "doing the drive or the *Concours*?" We didn't know what the *Concours* was and paid the fee for the drive. Almost an hour later, after winding along the two-lane road lined with enormous homes, we were forced to stop because there was a procession of vintage cars waiting to enter The Lodge at Pebble Beach. I quickly jumped out of the car and ran to the median to "*ooh*" and "*aah*" at the beautiful old cars. A brilliant blue one caught my eye. They were all breathtaking, but this BMW was one of the most spectacular automobiles I'd ever seen.

"Nice car," I casually threw out to the driver. He smiled and said, "Thanks." He told me about the BMW and then I asked him about the procession. He explained that it was the *Concours d'Elegance*, an annual competition which drew the finest vintage automobiles from all over the country. He looked familiar and I asked him if we had met before. He smiled and said that he didn't think so. My husband, who had come up and was standing some distance behind me, looked horrified. The fellow and I continued to chat and again I asked, "Are you sure we haven't met before?" Once again he shook his head no. We talked on as the cars began rolling into the grounds of The Lodge. As we were commenting on the different ones, it suddenly dawned on me who he was, and I gasped, "Oh, my God!"

"Shhhh," he pleaded, looking around quickly to see if any other spectators had heard my exclamation. As my mouth gaped open, he applied the gas and slipped easily through the gates into the *Concours*. I looked around at my husband who was shaking his head in disbelief. I never even asked if it was because he was embarrassed or just plain surprised at my stupidity.

I didn't care. As we walked back to our car and discussed finding a restaurant for dinner, I smiled. We had been in Monterey for less than two hours and already I had spent ten minutes chatting with Clint Eastwood.

Maybe, just maybe, this Army thing was going to be OK.

As an Army wife, BETTY VORIS served on the boards of OWC, was post volunteer coordinator for the American Red Cross, and chair for ten years of "Take Christmas to the VA Hospital." Using her professional name, Betty Packard has been a reporter, magazine editor, publisher, teacher, continuing education specialist, public speaker, and consultant. In 2006, the National Federation of Press Women awarded her their highest honor, National Communicator of Achievement. She and her husband Steve live in San Francisco but travel often to visit their three children, eight grandchildren and five great-grandchildren.

Dress Mess
JANINE BOLDRIN

As a young lieutenant in the Army, my husband often came home with an invitation for us to attend events. The get-togethers ranged from casual socials to formal dinners, but I was usually clueless on the details until the last minute.

With such little information, I often made bad decisions about what to wear, at least to those first events. I wore shorts to my first coffee and was greeted by cute sundresses. There was the night I wore a skirt and blouse to a Hail and Farewell, only to be told while we were in transit that it was a college-themed barbecue. And I also made the mistake of wearing a cocktail dress to a formal event where I spent the entire evening looking out of place among a sea of floor-length gowns.

My clothing choices weren't a major issue, just slightly embarrassing to a new Army wife who wanted to look appropriate for the occasion. So when my husband told me we were going to attend a ceremony where one of his soldiers would receive an award from the Royal Rangers, a church-based Boy Scout-type group, I knew to ask early on what I should wear.

My husband came home the next day with the answer. He should wear his dress blue uniform and I should wear something formal. I was surprised, but my husband insisted the soldier said it was a formal event; besides, the award was for saving a child from drowning so the ceremony was probably a big deal.

That weekend, I worked my hair into a formal style, meticulously applied make-up, donned a tea-length, deep green slip dress, and added some shimmering drop earrings to finish the look. With my husband in his dress blues, I thought we looked pretty sharp. But as we pulled into the parking lot, I asked my husband again about what we were wearing. I knew he was starting to get annoyed by the question, but I had made the clothing mistake one too many times to do it again.

At the door, we were greeted by a smiling young man in his Class A uniform who was very pleased to see his platoon leader. I could tell by the look in the soldier's eyes that this was an important night for him. And that is the only reason I didn't turn and run out when we walked into the gym and found people seated at the round tables wearing jeans and Royal Ranger uniform shirts.

I flashed a panicked look at my husband, but he kept his cool as we were ushered over to where we would be sitting for our meal. I couldn't believe we were wearing formal clothes at such a casual affair. As we sat at the table, I caught glimpses of people looking our way. My husband and I were quiet as we walked up to get our meals, but I was sure that by this time he was as uncomfortable as I was.

Just as we picked up our utensils to eat, an older gentleman walked over to us and sat down at our table. "I want to tell you how nice it is to have you here tonight." He wore a cap that proudly displayed his status as an Army Veteran. "And you look great. You really look great."

He spent time talking to us about his experience in the military and about how much he missed being a soldier. More people came over and talked to us, many commenting on how much they enjoyed seeing my husband's uniform. In the end, everything worked out for the best. And maybe our dressing up added just a little something to a very important night.

But I did learn my lesson. I don't rely on my husband for details on appropriate dress at our events anymore. As soon as an invitation comes in, I call another wife and ask *her* what to wear.

JANINE BOLDRIN is the managing editor of *Military Spouse* magazine and former editor of *Military Kids' Life* magazine. She was an Army wife for 20 years. Janine lives with her three children in the Hudson Valley.

Tacos with a Side Order of Foot-in-the-Mouth
ANNA GIBBONS

My husband, Tom, and I had only been married two weeks before we settled into a little apartment in Clarksville, Tennessee. It was a small place behind a roller rink and close to Fort Campbell where he was a first lieutenant.

As a new wife from a civilian area in upstate New York, everything about military life was new and difficult for me. One time I forgot my ID card so I couldn't get into the commissary. When I told Tom what happened, he flipped out.

"You have to keep that ID card with you at all times!" he emphasized, a little louder than necessary. It was the first time I'd heard that I needed to carry that beige card *everywhere*.

"I'm just not used to this," I thought. Simple errands like grocery shopping were unfamiliar and awkward. Even going to the doctor was different. I'd seen the same family doctor all my life. Now I called a clinic and got an appointment with a total stranger.

Within a few weeks an invitation came for a Brigade Welcome Coffee. That was two more new things: I didn't know what a "welcome coffee" was, and I didn't know what a "brigade" was. The company commander's wife, whom I'd met, assured me it would be fun, so I arranged to meet her at the Mexican restaurant which was not far from our apartment.

I arrived before her and I was a little uncomfortable because I didn't know anyone else. As I shifted from foot to foot, a striking woman came up and introduced herself. I felt a little underdressed next to her because she was really well put-together—almost larger than life with beautiful blonde hair and pageant-ready looks. She must have sensed I was a newcomer because she skillfully drew me into conversation with her soft Southern accent.

Before I knew it I was going on and on about the events of the past month and how hard it was getting used to this life. I told her I was new to the south and new to the Army. My family had no exposure to the military at all. I'd lived in the Northeast all my life. Even the food in Tennessee was different.

My new friend listened sympathetically. She was easy to talk to and very down-to-earth, which is why I felt comfortable opening up to her. I figured she must be the wife of a captain or a major in the brigade.

When the cocktail hour ended, we all moved to another room for dinner. I sat down at a table with her and some other women. Then, figuring I had done most of the talking, turned and asked her a question.

"What does your husband do?" I said loud enough that the whole table heard.

She didn't say anything for a moment or two. The group became silent and everyone stared at me in horror.

She put her hand on mine and said in her peaches-and-cream voice, "Honey, my husband is the commanding general of Fort Campbell."

You could've heard a pin drop. I was so embarrassed! I had been chatting with the general's wife for half an hour and didn't even know it. I felt like the bottom had just dropped out of the restaurant.

Luckily, the battalion commander's wife was sitting on the other side of me and put her arm around me protectively. Leaning toward the general's wife, she explained, "Anna is a new wife. She doesn't know the chain of command yet."

I wanted to crawl under a rock, but the general's wife put me at ease.

"Anna, you flattered me," she insisted, smiling. "Imagine, thinking I was young enough to be a captain's wife. What a compliment!"

The other ladies at the table laughed off my social gaffe in a way that didn't make me feel like I wanted to run out of the room. Before long even I was chuckling.

The division commander's wife and I built a friendship out of that shaky first meeting. Afterwards, whenever we were at the same function, she made it a point to come over and say hello. I'm sure I was indelibly imprinted on her memory for good reasons, just as I'll always remember her for her beauty and graciousness.

I learned two things from that embarrassing moment. First, we're all just human. And second, when you don't know anything about the military, boy is it hard!

ANNA GIBBONS is a fitness instructor, personal trainer, and bodybuilder. She and her husband Tom have two adult children and live in Rhode Island.

It's All About the Dress
LINDA EBERHARTER

Military balls—the ones that are mandatory to attend—are no big deal for the service member. They buy a set of dress blues and wear them every time. Not so for the military wife. These functions require an evening gown.

My husband, Lou, and I were stationed in Europe during the 80s. This was before the Internet, email, and buying online. For shopping we had few choices: the PX, a catalog, or the local economy stores.

Our second European tour was in Coevorden, The Netherlands, with the Combat Equipment Battalion Northwest, which was then known as a POMCUS ("prepositioning of material configured to unit sets") site. Lou oversaw the quality assurance for work the Dutch nationals performed on the equipment. It was considered a remote site with only 15 American families in the immediate area. We had wonderful homes specifically constructed for the American military, but for everything else we had to fit ourselves into the local community. The town was small (15,000) with shops, great restaurants, and one bank. The Dutch residents enjoyed having the U.S. military present, and we each shared our traditions. At Christmas, we adopted their December Fifth arrival of the Dutch *Sinterklaas* on a boat from Spain, and their children joined ours for trick-or-treat on Halloween.

One large, old house had been converted into what services we had. There was a lending closet (situated in a room which probably had been a closet in the house), a small PX, a Religious Education office, the University of Maryland office, and a mini-library. Our kids, if they were in high school, took a bus to the nearest Department of Defense high school, which was 90 minutes away. Yes, you can say it was remote.

The few military balls we had were larger events done in combination with other battalions from as far south as Brussels, Belgium, so there were more than 15 couples at these functions. The local stores did not carry the evening gowns appropriate for these functions. What was available was more suited to a night out in a club. Even the large PX near the high school was small in comparison to most, so to say there were slim pickings in evening gowns was an understatement.

Some of the ladies traveled to the larger, northern Germany Army installations for their gown quests. I opted for the catalog.

I fell in love with a dress from a picture. It was a teal blue, long column dress with an overlay of chiffon. I filled out the order form, sent in my check, and waited patiently. Six weeks later it finally arrived. It was as pretty on as it was in the catalog, and it fit great except for the length. I'd need some high, high heels.

None of my shoes had high enough heels, and nothing I found in town worked either. The ball was coming up, so there was no time to order a pair or travel to find something appropriate. I wore what I had, knowing the dress would drag the ground. Maybe walking on tiptoes would work.

I was confident that I'd be the only woman wearing this dress. It can be a problem when living in places where selection was limited; someone else inevitably showed up wearing the same dress you wore. Yet, I was sure that wouldn't be the case, and even more assured when, upon arriving and quickly scanning the other ladies, I didn't see any teal gowns anywhere.

Lou was behind me as we joined the receiving line that snaked up a wide staircase to meet the commanding general and his wife. When we were nearly at the top, he took another step up and said into my ear, "Looks like there is someone else here with your dress."

As I quickly turned to look down the stairs at the foyer, I didn't see another teal gown, but I definitely felt a rip at the waistline of mine. My husband was standing on the hem of my dress as it dragged along the floor. "Oh no! You just tore my dress!" I hissed into his ear. He looked, and sure enough, there was a four-inch rip in the back.

"Now what?!" I asked as the line moved again. We couldn't just stay where we were.

"Let's just keep moving," he whispered. "I'll put my hand there to cover it."

I took the final step up and heard the fabric rip again. He was still standing on the hem! I glared at him. "Let's get this over with," I mumbled as he finally moved off the hem. We shuffled awkwardly through the receiving line, smiling when we needed to smile, and then I quickly backed up against the closest wall and sent Lou to find a few safety pins.

After completely removing the dress in the restroom stall to pin the waist together, I re-combed my hair, touched up my lipstick, and made my way back to my husband. As we headed to our assigned table, I ran into one of my good friends.

"Love your dress, Linda," she said. "I haven't seen one like it tonight. I've seen mine three times."

"I think Lou saw someone with this same dress," I said. "I was distracted and didn't spot it." I just hoped the pins wouldn't pop and puncture my skin.

Just then, Lou grabbed my hand and said, "Over there, the lady by the far window." I looked and saw a gal in a long, royal blue gown, similar in lines to mine, but definitely not the same.

"Oh, that dress isn't anything like mine dear," I purred. He squinted and looked again, finally admitting it wasn't the same.

"I have to get my eyes checked," he said, shaking his head.

I survived that night, even danced and not once did I get stuck by a pin. However, since you can't wear the same dress to another function, this one was packed away, pins and all. We had a good laugh about that evening some years later when we ran across the dress during one of our throw-out cycles in preparation for a move. I still loved the teal color though. Maybe, I thought, my Mom could mend it properly and I'd save it for my daughter one day, that is, if she ever happened to attend a military ball with her service member husband. Somehow, I doubted it would double as a senior prom dress.

LINDA EBERHARTER works in the IT division of a large Veterans organization and owns an online publishing business. Her life as an Army wife led her to Indianapolis, Indiana, where she still calls home. She has two children, now both grown and living in sunny Florida.

Queen of Everything
ELLIE KAY

Every year at Holloman Air Force Base, two flying squadrons bring out a dozen sleek black F-117A fighters and set them out on the flight line ramp. The area between two sets of specially designed hangars that house the F-117s is called "The Canyon." The pilots' wives were going to have their annual photo shoot in front of these awesome jets, and it was no laughing matter. These women took this photo-op seriously, and I was about to discover just how serious. We were instructed to wear white T-shirts, blue jeans, black boots, and brown bomber jackets (borrowed from our hubbies). We dubbed ourselves the Blue-Jeaned Stealth Queens as we strutted our stuff in front of the jets. Never mind the fact that all together we had 48 kids, 187 loads of laundry, and 67 dogs waiting for us at home. We were proud that we still had "it." The only problem was, most of us couldn't remember where we put it.

I was excited about being a Stealth Queen. Hey, I'd been called the "Coupon Queen" and the "Savings Queen" for years. Why couldn't I just be Queen of Everything? So I thought royalty could slide on the dress code a bit: instead of the mandatory white T-shirt, I had an ecru-colored shirt on. I thought the jacket would cover it and no one would notice. I was wrong.

When we were ready to walk out with the photographer, a mean-eyed mama thrust a white T-shirt under my nose and hissed, "Quick, put this on; that ecru-colored shirt will ruin the overall effect."

Now is a good time to mention an important fact about a certain limitation I have. You see, when God passed out common sense, he gave my friend Myra a double portion and reduced my part to a morsel.

So I stood there looking at the guys on the flight line. The entire crew was resting in the shade by the jets. There were no bathrooms nearby, and the mean-eyed mama was staring at me with her lips tensed, tapping her foot. How in the world was I going to take off my ecru shirt and change into the white T-shirt in front of God and country and mechanics?

My thoughts were interrupted by a tap on my shoulder. It was common-sense Myra. "Ellie, you could just slip the white T-shirt over the shirt you're wearing now," she said.

"Uh, yes, of course," I stammered, wondering why I hadn't thought of the obvious.

I quickly pulled on the white T-shirt and then found myself faced with yet another dilemma. You see, when a woman has had a basketball team's worth of children, there's a basic problem. I was wearing "Great Shapes" No Nonsense panty hose. (They guarantee to take five pounds off any figure.) In fact, I was wearing two pair to remove that extra ten pounds.

There was no way I could leave that shirt untucked, or the added bulk would make me look like a buffalo in that there canyon. Once again my hero, Myra, came to the rescue. "Here, Ellie, Marcie and I will hold up our jackets while you tuck your shirt in."

What a relief!

The two women held up their jackets, shielding the view from the flight-crew members by the jets.

I quickly dropped my pants low enough to neatly tuck in my shirt and pulled them up again. With a sigh of relief, I zipped the jeans and turned around to pick up my jacket from the pavement. At that moment I saw an awful sight.

To my utter embarrassment, I noticed, for the first time, a row of twelve men sitting in the shade of the hangar about two hundred yards behind me. The girls shielded the view of the guys in front of us, but no one saw the crowd behind us.

Myra noticed the peeping toms at the same time I did and was quick to comfort me with "Hey, Ellie, don't worry about it. I don't think they even noticed."

Momentary relief accompanied my hope that maybe Myra was right and they hadn't noticed. I slowly stole a side-glance at the group sitting in the shade.

They were waving at me, slapping each other on the back, and laughing.

ELLIE KAY is the founder and CEO of Heroes at Home, a 501(c)(3) that provides financial literacy to military members. Author of fifteen books, popular speaker, corporate educator, spokesperson, and mother of seven children, she's married to Bob Kay, a former Stealth fighter pilot. Her bestselling paperback, *Heroes at Home* (now in its third printing), has been distributed to military families around the world under a presidential initiative. In 1998 she received the Army's highest civilian medal, the Dr. Mary E. Walker Award, for outstanding dedication to improving the quality of life for soldiers and their families. Find out more at www.Elliekay.com. ("Queen of Everything" is reprinted with permission from *Heroes at Home: Help and Hope for America's Military Families* by Ellie Kay [Bethany House, a division of Baker Publishing Group, 2002].)

Cats and Bats

He's Thinking Arby's
TARA CROOKS

Kevin and I got married during college and our first home was an apartment. My husband and I are both dog lovers but an apartment wouldn't allow for dogs, so we decided on a cat. We headed down to the local Humane Society. I'm a softy and I know that everyone will adopt the kittens, so I headed straight back to the older cats. Unfortunately, my husband wasn't interested in an older cat. He chose a scraggly, skinny, black kitten that was about three months old. I argued with him for half an hour against this cat, but he had made up his mind.

We took ol' "blacky" home with us and named him Oscar. It didn't take long for us to realize that Oscar was no ordinary cat—he was a super cat. Once he mastered the apartment itself he started hanging out on the deck. We were on the third floor of the apartment complex so it never occurred to us the cat would try to escape, but he did. Six months into our family of three, we posted "Lost Cat" signs all over the complex hoping to find him. Lucky for him he wore a collar and was returned several days later.

Our time in college flew by. My husband graduated from Reserved Officer Training Corps (ROTC), and we headed to our first duty station at Fort Hood, Texas. We found a wonderful little rental house (with a cat door) on a cul-de-sac. Oscar fit right in. He immediately claimed the entire cul-de-sac as his territory and started visiting the neighbors. It wasn't long before all the children knew his name. He took up a perch in the neighbor's tree with a bird's eye view of the area. He caused most of his mischief there. The birds loved this tree and he loved the birds. Maggie, our neighbor, put birdseed in the feeder; Oscar waited for the hungry birds and then brought the ultimate prize to our doorstep. Maggie wasn't appreciative. While we knew it was a gesture of love, bird carcasses aren't exactly something you like to find when you step outside your front door.

Days would go by and we'd never see Oscar. When we asked if anyone had seen him, we'd find him curled up on the back of our friend Jennifer and Tim's couch. "Oh, he's been here for two days. What a sweet cat," they said. Boy, did he have them fooled!

Teresa and Patrick across the street owned Oscar's two best friends, the Doberman Pinschers. Teresa called me all the time to tell me how my cat was purposely walking on top of her fence and jumping down into the "pit" of dogs, then running diagonally across the yard to see if they'd catch him, causing her dogs to throw giant barking fits. She was worried Oscar would be eaten until we decided they were all friends and this was just a game they played.

At Fort Hood, Oscar survived the Dobermans, Maggie spraying him out of the tree with the water hose, the children burning his leg on the barbecue grill, and even a bout of kidney failure. The veterinarian said we owned a miracle cat. By the time I brought him in for treatment, he said most cats would have been dead. We thought Oscar had seen enough adventure in his life. That is, until we made our next major move.

After leaving Fort Hood we spent eight months at the Captain's Career Course in Fort Sill, Oklahoma, followed by a year unaccompanied tour to Korea during which our daughter Wrena and I moved to Springfield, Missouri. After returning from Korea, Kevin had orders to report to Fort Stewart, Georgia. We went through all the motions: the movers, the partial DITY move, the goodbyes to the family, and the packing of the plants, pets, and kid.

We headed off on the 16-hour trip to Georgia—a car and a truck pulling a U-Haul trailer. We stopped in Alabama at an Arby's to have lunch. Since Oscar had been riding in his cage the entire way we decided it would be nice to let him out in the back of the Durango. We left the windows barely—and I do mean barely—cracked for air. Upon returning to the vehicle, I opened the door. I looked around. No cat. I started to freak out. No cat? How could there be no cat? We combed that truck from one end to the other. He was gone. I was beside myself. We spent the next hour driving around the parking lots of adjacent restaurants calling for him. Kevin finally said we had to go. "You never leave a soldier behind," I told him, crying as we drove away.

I started thinking of ways to rescue him. Did he have a collar on? Yes! What was on it? I don't know. It could have been Texas, Oklahoma, or Missouri. I couldn't remember. I did remember slipping it on him right before we left so that if he got lost someone would know his name and he would have a family. I don't know how, but I recalled the vet's name and number from Texas, and from Missouri, and our old phone number from Oklahoma. I called all the numbers and told them my story.

Two days after we arrived at Fort Stewart, we met the movers at our rental house and my cell phone rang. "Hello," said a woman's voice. "Are you missing a member of your family?" The lady explained she was in Leeds, Alabama. Our Oscar had been found! She said her daughter found him by the dumpster at Arby's and the only reason she took him home was because he had a collar. Once she got him home it took her two days to figure out why the cat was in Alabama with a Missouri and Texas vet tag and an Oklahoma phone number. Only in a military household! She had called the vet in Texas who gave her my number. What an amazing woman with a huge heart to not only take him in but to spend so much time finding his family. I was so appreciative and happy to know Oscar had been rescued. On the other hand, now that I knew he was safe, I was totally irritated with him for jumping out. The next weekend, we drove 12 hours to bring him home.

I don't know how he is so lucky. Since he's been back, we purchased a nice home in Richmond Hill, Georgia. He has taken to our street and our neighbors just like he did in Texas. He scratches when he needs to go out, uses his cat door, and even has a self-feeding cat bowl. He is low maintenance but still very loving and has turned out to be a great cat. Though he is 13 years old now, he still goes on his adventures. We lost him around New Year's Day last year and some lady called from a neighborhood about ten miles away—ironically right down the street from the local Arby's.

TARA CROOKS, known as "The Oprah of the Armed Forces," has been a featured military family life expert in *Military Times, Stars and Stripes, USAA Magazine,* Military.com, and Army.com. She is co-founder of Army Wife Network (AWN) and producer of Army Wife Talk Radio, a coauthor of *1001 Things to Love about Military Life* (Hachette, 2011), 2013 Armed Forces Insurance™ Army Spouse of the Year, and American Legion Woman of the Year 2009. Tara "retired" from her military role in 2015 and passed on the legacy of AWN. She is currently an elementary school teacher living in Texas with her two daughters, Wrena and Chloe.

Blame It On Rio
NORA CARMAN

It all started when the Brazilian pharmacist handed me a small satchel of sedatives. We were preparing for our long journey home from Rio de Janeiro. We had spent a wonderful and wild year and a half in the luminescent country of Brazil. My husband had studied alongside the Brazilian Army at their Command and General Staff College as part of his training as a Foreign Area Officer. The city is amazing, terrifying (principally while trying to drive or cross the street) and beautiful all at once. Driving in Brazil took the nerves of Evel Knievel and a certain disregard for your life that enabled you to even sit behind the wheel. I possessed neither, and so used public transportation, the larger the bus the better. Now it was time to return to the American Midwest, the complete opposite of our current home. We would miss much about Rio, but were looking forward to calm Kansas.

I was exhausted. Movers normally finished our household packing in two or three days. This Brazilian company, however, dragged it out for a week. Two days before we were to fly out of the country, they were nowhere near completion, despite several calls to the manager. After I pleaded my case that we just send them away, get some rest, and change our plane tickets, my husband replied, "This Band-Aid is coming off TONIGHT!" We were going to finish packing come hell or high water, or however much we had to bribe the building manager to allow us to continue packing out past the 8 p.m. deadline. We finally finished at 3 a.m. My husband stood on the streets of Rio and spray-painted our name on the crates containing our goods. The moving company didn't have the appropriate seals.

We crawled onto the one mattress left in the apartment and passed out. Before long, the doorbell rang. It was the moving team and they wanted us to buy them breakfast. We had fed and even given them bags of clothing for a week. My husband roared down the stairs and scolded them in Portuguese. I was positive we would never see our belongings again. Surely they would open the doors of the moving truck and sell everything on the streets of Copacabana. Later that day we shipped our car and packed for the flight.

You might be surprised to hear that the sedatives were for our two small, Brazilian-born kittens. I had never traveled with animals before and this was a long flight with a change of planes and about 15 hours of travel. The vet recommended that I carry the cats with me on the plane and give them a little something so they would sleep most of the flight. I had traversed a Kafkaesque maze to get all of their documents stamped for travel. This, combined with the $80 cost of each carrier and the $300 surcharge the airline required, endeared them all the more to my dog-loving husband. I was ready for rest; sedatives for the cats, a little wine for me, a movie and a meal, and we'd be in Kansas. I sank into the tiny plane seat and closed my eyes.

Around Sao Paolo, our plane took on more passengers and I noticed something awry. The soft-sided pet carriers tucked under the seats in front of us were moving. Not a little but a *lot*. All of the sudden, a rip appeared in the zipper and to my stunned, bleary eyes a kitty paw shot out of the carrier.

"Excuse me," I said frantically to the woman seated in front of me. "Could you put your seat up?" She had it reclined into my lap. "I need to get my carriers out from beneath your seat."

I grabbed the first case just in time to see the cat tear the zipper from its lining and force her little head out of the hole. Apparently these bags could withstand the antics of a four hundred pound ape but not my two cats. They had morphed into bionic kittens with super powers. I ran for the nearest bathroom, shut myself and the psycho kitty inside and locked the door. My husband was not far behind with the second carrier. Both cats looked crazed and had dismantled each case to escape. The flight attendants were none too happy that I had commandeered one of their restrooms on an international flight. My wonderfully pragmatic husband calmly explained that either they relinquish one of their eight lavatories or stand by as crazed cats ran rampant throughout their food service. I spent the nine-plus hour flight in the lavatory. This was no small feat for me as I'm a slight germaphobe and detest airplane facilities. Nevertheless, there I was, sprawled out on the toilet seat, feet propped up on the sink, trying to calm two extremely wigged-out cats. We had become "those passengers!!" I desperately wanted to wake up to discover it was all a nightmare. No such luck.

The airline phoned ahead to Atlanta to apprise them of the onboard situation. They arranged for a "cat lady" to meet us at the gate with a hard-sided carrier and double bolt lock. My husband, amazingly, had duct tape in his carry-on bag. What a prepared Army guy! We were able to tape together one carrier enough to stuff both cats in it and gracefully exit the plane.

Customs had been forewarned, too. "Welcome back to America. Heard you had a long flight," drawled the merciful attendant. "No, don't need to see anything," he said, as I dragged out a stack of stamped paperwork that had taken no small portion of my life to attain. "Move it along." No one wanted to let the cat out of the bag, literally.

We swiftly made it through customs and on to Kansas. There we retrieved the cats from baggage claim, although by this time they could not walk in a straight line. When we finally made it to the hotel, I collapsed on the bed with the bedraggled cats, their food and water beside me. I passed out in a pile of tears and uncontrollable laughter caused by stress. I was on the verge of moving mania.

When I finally awoke the next day, we went to the vet at Fort Leavenworth. He looked at the "sedative" we'd given the cats and I'll never forget his words: "I have to confiscate this drug and destroy it. This is a highly controlled psychotropic substance used only on psychotic adults. I have never seen it used on animals."

Our cats had experienced a hallucinogenic episode, a trip within a trip. My next question was intended as a joke. "Will they have flashbacks?" He studied the side of the bottle, looked up and said, "It's possible."

NORA CARMAN spent nearly 20 adventurous, challenging years as an Army wife. After 13 military moves, including Germany, Brazil, and the Mojave Desert, she, her husband, and their two children now call California home. She's part of a bible study that ministers to military wives in the area. Nora holds a BA in Literature and minor in Psychology from Wheaton College and a Master's in Public Health from NY Medical College. Among her favorite things are time with family and friends, long hikes, and finally feeling at home.

I Can Handle Just About Anything But That
ANDI HURLEY

Life was good. As good as it could be with a deployed husband. Spring was in full bloom. I had been productive all weekend. Checklists were under control. Things were accomplished. My husband would soon be home. At approximately 10 p.m. on Sunday evening, the cat began making a terrible chatter. I saw her on the sofa in the sitting area gazing up at the blinds. I knew immediately that there was a fly or a butterfly tucked in the blinds, and it was driving her crazy. I walked over, tapped the blinds and the intruder flew right at my head. It took less than one second to figure out this was not a fly but a *BAT!*

I immediately swung into action. I opened the deck door and grabbed a broom. *Get out of here*, I said to myself. The cat jumped from the buffet to the sofa to the table, the dog barked madly, and the bat flew around and around. I attempted to swat it with the broom, but it was too fast. It headed to the kitchen and I lost a visual on the intruder. I grabbed the phone and called the police. (No, I didn't call 9-1-1!)

"Do you do bats?"

"Bats?"

"Yes, I have a bat in my house and my husband is deployed. I'm not sure what to do."

"Ma'am, we'll send an officer over."

They lied. Not one, not two, but three police cars showed up at my house, lights flashing, no less. Three nice men rummaged through my things attempting to flush out the nasty creature. One of them told me this was only his second "bat call" in seven years. They tried to find it, but after 30 minutes, we all knew that it could be anywhere and there was nothing we could do about it. Asking the officers to stand guard all night wasn't an option, but I did consider it. Seriously.

I thanked the officers and apologized for wasting their time. I whipped off an email, though not frantic, to the husband, hoping he'd get a chance to read it early. I quickly threw some things in a bag, loaded the dog up, and headed to a hotel. (It cost me an arm and a leg because I had the dog with me.) We arrived at midnight shaken and tired.

After a few hours of sleep, the dog and I awoke and I called the "experts," those people in the phone book who advertise that they can remove squirrels, birds, snakes, and bats from your home. Thank God for "experts." When I arrived back at the house, the cat was on the sofa again, staring into the blinds, so I knew the nasty creature was back in his old spot. I opened the blinds slowly and my suspicion was verified. The bat was just "hanging out" as if this were *his* home. I left him alone, knowing that the expert would soon take care of the problem.

The expert arrived and said he needed to inspect the house. He went into the attic, came back down, and delivered the first good news in hours.

"There is no trace of other bats. Your attic is sealed tight. No bat droppings." He poked around the house some more and informed me that this was most likely a fluke; the bat must have come in when I opened the door (memo to self: don't leave the back door open at night ever again). Then, he delivered the blow: "As for the bat right there (pointed to nasty creature) there is nothing I can do. We specialize in flushing out several bats, not just one. I don't have tools to do that." My smile faded fast. "Call animal control," he said, and left.

I called. Animal control could cart off the nasty creature. One hour passed. Two hours. Three hours. The nasty creature was still hanging upside down in my house. I called them again.

"Well, right now we have a bear on the loose."

"Oh, and I thought I had problems."

"We'll be there as soon as we can, and if it's after dusk ..." Whatever was said after that, I didn't hear it. Expert had already told me that the nasty creature would hang there all day if I left him alone. He's sleeping. How nice. I'm starring in my own version of "Fear Factor" while nasty creature naps. But expert warned me that the nasty creature would awake at dusk and begin to fly.

I was not about to let that happen. I called a friend, another soldier who my husband had contacted earlier and asked to check on me. He came equipped with a net and heavy-duty gloves. The net was a nice concept, but bats have a way of slipping through the netting and I told my friend that we had one shot at this and no room for error. So, in the end, we sealed the deal using a perfectly lovely, plush blanket (now in the trash) that had previously adorned the loveseat. We threw the blanket over the intruder, trapping him, and then we took the package out the deck door and flung him over the railing. Unfortunately, he landed a bit too close to my property line, so I had my borrowed knight in shining armor go fetch the bat and take him far, far away. I don't care to know how far, exactly, only that it was far, far away.

Nasty creature removed. Removed from the blinds. Removed from the house. Removed from the property. I think the cat missed her playmate, but I sure didn't.

Some days I miss my husband more than others.

ANDI HURLEY'S husband recently retired from the U.S. Army, and they were thrilled to plant permanent roots in Florida. During their time as an Army family, they moved 15 times in 24 years. Andi now applies her experiences and creativity as a professional home stager to help owners prepare their properties for market.

Critter Jitters
JANINE BOLDRIN

Because the Army is notorious for locating posts in extreme climates, I have found there is one thing I can count on when we arrive at our new home.

Critters.

Soon after we move all of our furniture into just the right spot, and the boxes are put out on the sidewalk for pick-up, the critters come to welcome us.

At Fort Lewis, we woke up mornings to find big, fat slugs lounging on our sidewalks enjoying the gentle mist of the Pacific Northwest. They were slimy, squirmy banana-shaped things that camouflaged themselves in the concrete. It took only one barefoot trip out to get the newspaper to convince me that there was nothing worse than stepping on a slug.

Except sleeping with spiders. Washington State was a breeding ground for these little beauties too. They lurked in the corners of the house and bred entire armies of babies. As a new mom, I constantly checked for any signs of bites on my infant when I found spiders in our bed and crib.

Someone made the mistake of telling me that dangerous brown recluse spiders lived in the Pacific Northwest. An Internet search revealed that the only brown recluse found in Washington was from a trailer of household goods from Kansas. Could he have been a stowaway from a Fort Leavenworth PCS?

Our next move took us to Fort Benning, Home of the Infantry and of the cockroach. The house we were assigned had a huge, old tree out front where thousands of these creatures liked to hang out. Much to my dismay, they also liked to stop by and visit with our family on a daily basis.

Grossed out by the reputation of cockroaches, I enlisted my husband to do battle with the ugly bugs that were lurking inside our basement window well. He wrapped a scarf around his mouth and nose before lowering himself down into the hole with several cans of Raid. Later, he would describe the experience as something out of a horror movie when a swarm of cockroaches scurried past him to the safety of the tree as he unleashed that first can of spray.

Soon we packed our boxes, hoping they were critter-free, and drove to Fort Drum. The day we arrived in Watertown, New York, the weatherman reported the temperature at -10 degrees without the windchill, and forecasted that the temperature would drop throughout the week. Surely, no critter could survive these temperatures!

But my hope of having a creature-less existence was quickly dashed. Early Christmas Eve, my husband went down to our basement to retrieve a decoration from one of our boxes only to be surprised by an aerial attack.

Bats.

I spoke with friends who lived near us and they confirmed that Watertown was well known for these creatures. The big brown bats sometimes hibernated in buildings over the winter and liked to roost in confined, dark spaces like our attic during the summer. Armed with spray foam, my husband did his best to plug holes on the outside of the house to keep the bats from coming back while he was deployed. But a few months into his absence, I waged my own war with a scrappy little bat who liked the dark of my walk-in closet.

With our most recent move to North Carolina, I speculated on what new pest would become a part of my vocabulary. Again, it didn't take long to find out. As we settled down on the floor picnic-style to eat the first dinner in our new home, we unintentionally left some tasty crumbs for our new friends.

The ants welcomed us by throwing a party on our dining room floor the next day. I welcomed them by purchasing some ant hotels so they can be comfortable in our new home.

Next year, we will be moving again. Will we luck out and live in our first critter-free home? Who knows? But I am bringing Raid, spray foam, and a few mousetraps just to be safe.

JANINE BOLDRIN is the managing editor of *Military Spouse* magazine and former editor of *Military Kids' Life* magazine. She was an Army wife for 20 years. Janine lives with her three children in the Hudson Valley.

Cats on a Plane
ANGELA OWENS

Studies have suggested that pets can positively affect your well-being in numerous ways, from improving everyday happiness to increasing longevity. That's great. However, I'm pretty certain that theory goes out the window if you ever have to move your pets overseas!

When we moved to Vicenza, Italy, in the summer of 2003, we had only one pet, a lovable, if intellectually challenged, 100-pound golden retriever named Ranger. Preparing to bring him overseas involved endless paperwork and trips to specially certified veterinarians, all of which had to be completed within five days of flying. Really? Within five days of moving to a foreign country? What else could I possibly have to do?

When we arrived in Venice, I was clutching a thick file of Ranger's "bona fides" ready to vigorously defend my dog's health. Of course, given the general state of my luck in such matters and the exemplary state of my preparedness, we were waved through customs without so much as a glance at my paperwork masterpiece.

I promised never to do this to myself again. Somehow I'd get out of it when we left Italy. Maybe the rules would change. Maybe we'd never leave. Maybe, well you get the picture. I didn't want to endure the angst-ridden paperwork drill ever again.

Within 18 months of arriving in Italy, my "no paperwork" edict was long forgotten. We had added two cats, Lucky and Boo, to our family. I had never considered myself a cat person, but I was charmed by their complete affection-only-on-my-terms attitude. Ranger needed only the briefest of glances to get him excited and ready for some attention. In fact, Ranger seemed to suffer from what can only be called "reverse anorexia." He truly believed he was a tiny, ten-pound dog who could crawl onto your lap. On the other hand, the cats seemed indifferent to us. Compared to Ranger, the apathy was refreshing. While I never regretted getting the cats, I definitely questioned it. That would be because of Boo.

Boo was an average-looking calico cat. Nothing outstanding, no unusual markings, no exceptional size, nothing that would ever make you look twice. That is, not until you understood what was wrapped in this unassuming package. The amazing Boo, a cat that had many of the same skills humans have, quickly brought a new dynamic to our home. He was able to unlock doors and open cabinets and drawers; he even managed to lock himself inside my daughters' room on one occasion. In fact, I was certain that when we were all asleep, he walked upright, surfed the Net, and helped himself to a beer now and then. Nevertheless, we loved our trio of pets, Boo included, so in the spring of 2006, when we received orders sending us to Fort Polk, Louisiana, I grudgingly took on the dreaded paperwork again.

It was pretty much as I had remembered it; five days out, blah, blah, blah. There was the added twist of going through both the American and Italian systems for paperwork, the true test of my self-proclaimed fluency. (It turns out I'm not fluent.) The other difference was that I asked the vet for tranquilizers for my cats. Ranger had always traveled well. The cats, on the other hand, went insane each time they got in a car. I couldn't imagine what would happen to them in the belly of an aircraft for an overseas flight.

Finally, the day of our departure arrived. We left Vicenza at 4 a.m. in order to make our flight to the States: three pets in crates, countless luggage, and six people, including me, clutching my pet documents and pet tranquilizers. I should have recognized it as a bad omen when both cats barfed up the pills and actually spit them at me. Bravely or stupidly, I kept trying to get them to take the pills until all I had were two upset cats and a glob of disintegrated kitty meds.

Once at the airport, however, things went more smoothly. The lines were short, and we managed to check our luggage and pets without too much drama. It was the first real feeling of freedom I'd had in weeks. After living out of suitcases and dealing with all the moving stress, and yes, the pet paperwork, all I had to do was sit back and relax until we arrived in Houston.

Our journey was scheduled to take us from Venice to Frankfurt, and then from Frankfurt to Houston. Upon arriving in Frankfurt, we didn't deplane through a jet way. Instead, we taxied to a designated spot and disembarked down portable stairs to the tarmac, where we were met by a bus to take us to the terminal. As we descended the stairs, the belly of the plane was opened to unload the luggage. Out of the corner of my eye I saw something that looked like Boo; in fact, it looked like Boo jumping from the belly of the plane onto the tarmac. Impossible! Boo was secured in a brand new crate. The crate had a locking mechanism and you needed opposable thumbs to open it. I shook my head. Apparently, early-onset jet lag and stress were making me hallucinate. Unfortunately, my daughters have greater faith in their senses. They immediately believed what they, too, saw.

Let me interrupt here. I was in the Army for five years, two of them on airborne status at Fort Bragg. One of the things I remember very clearly is that you do not mess with Air Force runways. You do not step onto them without proper clearance and an escort. I was fairly certain of two things. One, civilian runways were probably similar; two, I had no desire whatsoever to find out. That knowledge kept me rooted in place as I watched my real live cat, NOT my hallucination, dart across the Frankfurt runway. My daughters, caring only about their beloved Boo and not schooled in the finer aspects of runway etiquette, took off full speed onto an international runway. My husband and sons, not having seen Boo's escape, watched in disbelief as I then did what any mother would do: blew off the law and ran after my girls.

Needless to say, close on my heels was a contingent of weapons-toting security personnel. Oddly enough, it's not every day that you have three American females sprinting across your runway. Here's a fun fact: "Halt!" is the same in English and German.

This is where it gets a little muddled. From what I can piece together, my husband and two sons fell into the cat parade on the heels of the security people. Of course, while chasing us, my husband was probably contemplating the state of German jails and wondering how the words "international incident" would look on his record.

Then Boo just stopped. He sat and began grooming himself nonchalantly. How nice for him. This caused my daughters and me to stop abruptly. In fact the whole cat parade looked like a slapstick comedy as our human accordion crumpled. About this time, the security people began piecing together what had happened. However, no one was sure what to do, how to do it, who to yell at, and most importantly, who was in trouble. (I was not above letting the cat take the fall.) Finally, a brave baggage handler walked up to Boo, picked him up, and brought him back to us.

I wish I could say we all had a good laugh at this point, that all the participants in our twisted drama shared a comic moment that transcended language and cultural barriers. Sadly, I would be lying. The "no harm, no foul" philosophy wasn't making headway. I don't speak German ("halt" notwithstanding), but I did learn a few new vocabulary words, hand gestures included, that don't bear repeating. There were lots of questions and even more attempted explanations. Despite the language differences, we resolved the situation once everyone calmed down. Boo was back in his crate, and we got on the bus. "Quickly," I urged my family, "before they change their minds." Boarding the bus, we were treated to a round of applause, having been the best entertainment anyone had seen in a while. We then proceeded to the terminal and our connecting flight to Houston, with me wishing I had taken the kitty tranquilizers myself.

Amazingly, Boo did not have another transatlantic escape attempt. We arrived in Houston to find him in customs, asleep in his crate. My paperwork, once again, was not given the attention it deserved. But I was just happy to have my family and pets safe and free from incarceration. Boo's crate had been modified, however. It had been duct-taped into oblivion with only a few small air holes. There was also a note written in German with lots of capitalized letters, underlining, and exclamation points.

Sometimes I'm glad I don't read German.

ANGELA OWENS is a former Army officer and the spouse of a retired soldier. She and her husband live and work in Italy where they enjoy travelling as much as they can now that they are empty nesters. Despite living there for the last seven years, she is told her Italian is "surprisingly bad."

It Was A Dark and Stormy Night

It Was a Dark and Stormy Night
PHYLLIS DENTON

As I lay in bed listening to the rain pelt the house and the wind rattle the windows, the television scroll confirmed we were under a tornado warning. It was late May 1970 and we lived at Altus AFB in Oklahoma. Since we were smack in the middle of the famed Tornado Alley, the local weather folks conscientiously monitored conditions and kept us informed—and we always paid attention.

I was the only parent in our house that night with our five daughters, all under the age of nine. Earlier that day, my husband, a C-141 pilot, along with most of the other flight crews had answered an alert to fly all the aircraft to other bases in "safe" locations in other states and to stay there until the weather danger passed. Altus was the Air Force "schoolhouse" and there were plenty of expensive cargo planes on base, including the new C-5A. The irony didn't escape me though, that while the planes and crews might be safe, all the wives and children were left to fend for themselves during a very uncertain night.

As base houses went, ours was pretty good. It was a single story ranch home made of brick—a far cry from the sub-standard, low bid construction, sorry-excuse-for-a-house we'd lived in before. Since we had so many children, we were assigned roomy, four-bedroom quarters. Fortunately, there was a large closet in the hallway where we had been instructed to take shelter during tornado warnings.

Outside, the thunder crashed, lightning flashed, and rain splashed off the roof. As I contemplated the storm, the tornado siren on base sounded, just as I knew it would. One of the sirens was located at the base elementary school yard just a block away, so there was no mistaking it or sleeping through it. Through all the wind, it sounded like an air raid horn.

I slid out of bed and padded down the hall to the closet. Earlier that evening I'd emptied it of the laundry hamper and vacuum and various other items I stored there. It was a double closet with two sliding doors, enough room for all of us, barely. I arranged couch cushions and extra blankets and pillows on the floor to make it more comfortable. Realizing I'd forgotten a flashlight, I darted to the kitchen to get one, in case the power went out, as it threatened to. Then I went to the first bedroom and gently woke up my two oldest daughters, ages seven and nine. One by one, I carried their sleepy bodies to the closet. I did the same with the next two daughters, ages five and four. Once I had collected all of them, I retrieved the baby from her crib and climbed into the closet myself.

The six of us huddled in the cramped and dark space, the safest place in the house, all things considered. But I don't believe there is really a safe place when a tornado visits. Feeling vulnerable and alone, I sure wondered what my husband and the other pilots were doing at that moment. Probably they'd finished their steak dinners and were still at the Officers Club bar having drinks. I was normally pretty brave about things Air Force life threw at me, but that night I was genuinely frightened and alone. Five little faces looked up at me so I pretended not to be afraid as I snuggled them closely, tucked blankets around them, and urged them to go back to sleep. The younger girls eventually settled into slumber but the older ones stayed up with me. We talked, read books and sang songs to pass the time, until they were all asleep at last.

Outside, the police sound trucks moved about the housing area, blasting out urgent warnings through that tinny megaphone: "TORNADO SIGHTINGS. TAKE SHELTER IMMEDIATELY. REPEAT. THIS IS A TORNADO WARNING." Every few minutes the warnings repeated as the trucks criss-crossed the neighborhoods. Everything was chaotic and noisy and it felt like we were under attack.

In the past when the tornado siren summoned us to find shelter, we mostly just had to go inside our homes and stay there until the "ALL CLEAR" sounded. This was different; when that sound truck boomed "TAKE SHELTER" they really meant "in the closet."

During that storm, we stayed in the shelter all night waiting and hoping for calm. By the morning light, we still hadn't heard the "ALL CLEAR" signal. We needed food and bathrooms so I ventured first out of the closet and, seeing the stillness, felt certain the danger had passed.

Before long the sound trucks passed, assuring us conditions were once again safe. In the morning light, they reminded me of the ice cream truck, less threatening than the ominous, booming tones in the dark of the night. Still, I shuddered at the memory.

We filed out of our cramped, makeshift shelter, sleep-deprived, stiff, weary and somewhat stunned. Despite the terrifying events of the night before, school went on as usual, and the forecast promised sunshine and warm temperatures. In fact, the sky that day was the sharpest, brightest blue I'd ever seen in Oklahoma.

It was all over the news that 12 tornados had been sighted in Jackson County, *our county*, that night—12! But my husband had to take my word for it when he and the other crews flew the planes home later that day. By then there was only a solitary remnant looming perilously over the school playground—a huge white cumulus cloud whipped into a fluffy funnel shape, a testament to that very real, and very scary, dark and stormy night.

PHYLLIS DENTON is proud to say that of her five daughters, four are married to the military and three of them were active duty members themselves. She now lives in Las Cruces, New Mexico, where she often plays host to visiting family, which now includes 11 grandchildren.

The Safest Aisle in the Commissary
LISA SWEET

I had just gotten married and, after a few months of tying up loose ends at my job in New York City, I made the trek to Fort Rucker, Alabama. I moved into my first home in nearby Enterprise and as soon as I was carried over the threshold, I started preparing, but not the way most brides prepare. Yes, I unpacked my crystal and other wedding gifts, but I went into full-blown disaster preparedness! I created a kit replete with water bottles, radio, flashlight, snacks and more (kept in my interior bathroom). Much to my husband's chagrin, I purchased a weather radio that transmitted any major weather systems coming our way at all hours of the day (and night).

You see, I was frightened of tornados. I'd seen the movie *Twister* and of course *Storm Stories* on the Weather Channel, so I knew what I was up against. Coming from the Northeast, I never had to deal with tornados, except for a few rogue twisters in counties far from my home.

Despite my initial acute fears of severe weather phenomena in Alabama, after a few months of quiet days, I fell into a relaxed rhythm at Fort Rucker. I turned off the weather radio and pushed my fears to the back of my mind as I enjoyed new-lywed life, began a business, and took care of my new home. What a mistake! I should have remained on guard!

One sunny day—complete with puffy clouds floating lazily in a blue sky—I was in the commissary doing my weekly shopping. Just as I was about to join the check-out line, a huge storm rumbled in. Through the glass doors we watched the sky grow black, and everyone in the commissary perked up. *I hope I shut the windows in my car*, I thought. When I reached the cashier, I noticed people running back into the commissary! It was hailing! The lights flickered, then they went out completely.

Yes, I panicked, but really, it was a mild panic. *Surely this storm will pass*, I thought. The generator kicked in and we all breathed a sigh of relief as the reassuring beeps of the register resumed and the lights returned.

But then, everyone stopped and we all stared outside as the sky turned greenish black. I mean, it was a menacing color, the perfect shade of Wicked-Witch-of-the-West green. The manager announced over the loudspeaker, "We have just been informed that two, possibly three tornados have touched down in the area. The closest one is ten miles away. Please make your way to the back of the building. Again, please make your way to the back of the building. We will keep you apprised of any updates." I obeyed these orders immediately!

That fear of being swept up in a tornado took hold of me and I was terrified. Since I was new to the post, I didn't have the comfort of recognizing a single person in the commissary. When I realized my cell phone was in the car, I thought, "No last phone call to my husband. He'll just have to hear about me on the news." Yes, a tad over-dramatic, but I'm a weenie and not a Southern gal who can roll with the tornado "punches."

Then a sense of clarity came over me. I thought, *If this tornado hits, I shouldn't be in the back near the meat counter.* There'd be too many heavy food items flying around. No way should I be standing near the end-cap next to the canned soup either. Nervously but proud of my ingenuity, I made my way to the aisle with pliable, cushiony bread. If we got struck and shelves started falling, the bread would soften the blows.

I can happily report that as fast as the storm rolled in, it rolled out. I was a bit shaken, but managed to check out and even buy a pack of gum and the latest *People* magazine on the way out. I had many detours on the way home due to fallen trees blocking the roads, but when I returned, my visions of our house being destroyed quickly vanished. I was met at the door by my two hungry kittens, and I began unpacking my groceries (putting two cans of soup in my bathroom "safe room" just to be prepared). For a brief time after that storm, the weather radio stayed on and I'd huddle in the bathroom if I heard there was a "chance" or a "possibility" of "maybe" a storm nearby. But over time I relaxed and took it easy. We lucked out; there were no major storms to hit the area (except for a few hurricanes) for the remainder of our stay.

And that is how I learned my first lesson at Fort Rucker, one that I will gladly pass on to you: In the event of an emergency, go to the bread aisle, the safest aisle in the commissary.

LISA SWEET is the owner of BookThis! Inc., a boutique book and author PR agency. The agency travels wherever she and her husband—Zeke, an active duty Army officer—and three children, move. Currently they are avoiding tornadoes at Fort Leavenworth, Kansas.

Winter in Alaska with a Toddler
HEATHER L. WARD

Winter. In Alaska. With a toddler. Without my husband. Just typing those words makes me laugh! How in the world did a girl from South Jersey end up in this situation?

I consider myself to be an accidental military wife. I didn't grow up in a uniformed world and didn't purposefully set out to share my life with a soldier. We met and started dating while he was stationed at Fort Bragg, North Carolina, and I was living in Washington, DC. I didn't even understand the realities of my husband's career until I married him, and by then I loved him too much to back out.

In fact, before I met my husband, I had an image of "the perfect military wife" as someone who stood by her man and subjugated her own needs and wants. After years by my husband's side, I've learned that there is no perfect military wife, but those who seem to do it well have their own zest for life and an independent spirit. If I needed to literally stand by my man, I'd be a pretty lonely lady.

We arrived in Alaska at the tail end of the summer of 2004. I was five months pregnant with our first child. We thought we'd only be there for two or three years at most, just another stop on our road to other places. Chris, my husband, had returned from a year-long tour of duty in Operation Iraqi Freedom I (OIFI) in February of 2004. The unit we were joining at Fort Richardson in Alaska had just returned from Afghanistan in the summer of 2004, so I figured we'd avoid another deployment for a while. I hadn't planned on being in Alaska in October 2006 when the newly flagged 4-25th Brigade Combat Team set off for Iraq (with my husband as a patch-wearing member).

When I first heard of the impending deployment, my knee-jerk reaction was, "I am NOT staying in Alaska by myself with a two-year-old!" I told my husband to fly me anywhere but Fort Richardson. I seriously considered renting a house at the Jersey shore, within driving distance of my family, but not too close. (Living in Alaska has its advantages when your own family makes you crazier than the family you chose to create.) Normally, my motto is, "Home is where the Army sends me." But I had no desire to spend a winter cooped up with a toddler in Alaska. Alas, the Army won't move you just because your soldier deploys. When I considered the logistics of moving without Army funding, it seemed more stressful than remaining in Alaska. To my chagrin, I saw quite a few of my neighbors fly south for the deployment where they felt they had more support and warmer weather. It made me wonder if I was crazy to stay behind.

In keeping with Murphy's Law, the winter after my husband deployed was the snowiest since we moved to Fort Richardson. In January 2006, over 74 inches of snow fell in Anchorage, more than it normally gets all winter, and there were still four months of winter to go! On Valentine's Day, when my husband was away for a training exercise, I received a note from the housing office informing me that I had an "unauthorized amount of ice" covering my sidewalk and driveway. Prior to this, I had been uninvolved in snow and ice removal, thanks to being pregnant with my son and the rigors of caring for a baby. My husband took care of it. So, technically, the build-up of ice was his fault, but I was the only adult home when our nasty-gram arrived. I could have ignored it and let him take the fall, but something came over me and I became obsessed with getting rid of the thick slab of ice that surrounded our home. I quickly learned that chipping ice is really good exercise and a great way to take out my frustrations. As I chipped, I cursed and yelled and complained out loud; when I was finished (it took me several days to clear it all) I felt fabulous! I vowed to never have to chip ice like that again. I was going to learn how to prevent it from forming in the first place. I spotted a neighbor whose sidewalk was pristine and she passed her secret on to me. Astoundingly, if you shovel snow when it first lands and then douse your cement with ice melt, ice never forms!

During deployments, I took my job as the sole snow shoveler very seriously. We don't own a snow blower. Why buy one when both of my kindly neighbors have them? It also helps to have a gigantic vehicle in our driveway. My husband did what every red-blooded man does when he moves to Alaska: he bought a huge diesel truck with big tires. Unfortunately, this truck is a bit too much for me to operate, but it served a very useful purpose. It covered half our driveway so I didn't have to shovel as much!

Most importantly, I've also shattered my nightmare that I'd be cooped up in my house all winter, or rather my son shattered this vision. CJ was born here so this weather was fine and dandy with him. He had no idea there were fairer places we could be. So when the temperature reached double digits, we donned our winter gear and headed out to play in the snow. At first, I balked at all the preparation involved in a winter outing with a toddler, but when the temperature topped twenty degrees, it actually felt nice here, as long as we wore a down coat, snow pants, mittens, hat, and fur-lined boots. It used to take us about 30 minutes to prepare. Now we can be ready in about half that time. That's progress!

I loved watching CJ in his Army green snow suit, pulling his little blue sled behind him. (Being a true Army kid, he prefers to pull his own weight). During one of our regular snow walks, we managed to blaze a trail in the deep snow to his favorite neighborhood playground. For a while, we would just go view the play structure because it was nearly buried in snow. Recently, the snow began to melt and we were able to clear three out of four slides. It made me proud to watch him navigate the play structure in his bulky snow gear. While I originally worried that he'd be too fragile to handle the cold, I was the one who begged to go home. My hands and feet were numb.

I took him to the zoo on a "balmy" day in the high 20s and we had a ball. We took the sled in lieu of a stroller. We had been to the Alaska Zoo in the summer, but the cold-loving animals were actually more active in the winter. We visited his favorite animal, the musk ox (whom he referred to cutely as "m'gox") and marveled at Maggie the elephant's indoor treadmill to help keep her fit all winter long. Apparently, unlike CJ, she preferred to remain indoors in the winter. CJ loved the zoo in the winter so much that they had to ask us to leave at closing time; my son didn't want to go!

Just seeing the joy in his face—the parts that weren't covered by warm clothing—as he experienced winter in Alaska made staying there worthwhile. Now that winter is coming to an end and spring is just around the corner, I am so proud to know that I was able to make the best of a situation I once dreaded. And, amazingly, I cannot imagine how I ever would have made it through the winter in Alaska without my toddler.

HEATHER WARD has been a proud Army wife wince 1998. She has an MA in Counseling which has helped her survive two Iraq deployments. She has been privileged to serve as a Family Readiness Group Leader and is an Army Family Team Building Master Trainer.

Dodging Bullets
JACEY ECKHART

Now that our family has evacuated from the wildfires in San Diego, I'm pretty sure no one is going to let us move into their neighborhood. Ever. I'm pretty sure folks will check out our record of natural disasters and file a court injunction to keep us and THE BIG ONE away.

I can't blame them. No matter the duty station, we do seem to arrive right on time to be smack in the middle of one national disaster or another. We've done multiple hurricanes, including Katrina. We hunkered down in snow emergencies and catastrophic drought. The DC sniper even shot a lady at the Home Depot by our house in Arlington.

It's enough to make me think I'm cursed. Maybe I'm not actually wearing a chunky necklace from the sale bin at Kohl's, but the cursed amulet of an ancient Egyptian priestess who is darn mad about the weather.

My mom does not want to hear about any curses. Instead, the wildfires in San Diego made her more excited about my ability to evacuate and procure shelter than she was when I earned my diploma. "I hate to say that you're good at natural disasters," she gushed on the phone. "But, really, you are!"

Really, Ma, I'm not. More than anyone, I know our family's ability to squeak by during a disaster is not a certifiable skill. It's pure luck. Ask any one of the thousands of people who lost their homes. I swear this family is just dodging bullets.

Or at least that's what my 14-year-old tells me. "We gotta be like Neo in *The Matrix*," said Sam. "We bend and sway out of the line of bullets while the 3-D camera swings to a different angle."

I watched him demonstrate his *Matrix*-esque moves and thought that maybe the kid had something there. I don't mean that I'll be buying my son Neo's long leather trench coat complete with an arsenal stitched in the lining. I don't mean that I'll be dolling myself up in Trinity's molded body armor. All I meant is that I like Sam's idea about dodging bullets.

A lot of the time, that's what adult life—especially military life—is all about. Generally, we avoid disasters based on our own planning and common sense. We buckle our seatbelts. We stay off the top step of the ladder. We don't drink the Windex no matter what color it is. We buy insurance for everything else.

Yet there are moments when we're richly aware that no matter what we plan, we are really only dodging bullets. Time seems to slow and shift as we nip back into our own lane before that tractor trailer crosses the center line. The angles alter as we catch the baby as he launches himself out over a flight of stairs. The air crystallizes between bike tire and car bumper. That's the Neo moment when the bullet is dodged and tragedy passes. Then it's only an instant until everything speeds up again.

I'm OK with that. I don't need to be constantly aware of a world full of near-deaths and almost dangers. I just like to think that when these disasters pass us by we are meant to shift and bend and turn as Fate glides by swinging its awesome arsenal.

JACEY ECKHART is the author of the critically acclaimed book, *The Homefront Club: The Hardheaded Woman's Guide to Raising a Military Family* (Naval Institute Press, 2005) and the voice behind the award-winning CD *These Boots: A Spouse's Guide To Stepping Up and Standing Tall During Deployment*. She's been featured as a military family subject matter expert by the *New York Times*, NBC Dateline, CBS Morning News, CNN, NPR, the *Washington Post*, the *Washington Times*, *Woman's Day* magazine and many others. Her website is www.jaceyeckhart.net.

Family Planning,
Military Style

Unexpected Strength
DEBORAH LOGAN HORSTKOTTE

My husband was recently medically retired from the Navy. We were only married for two years of Joe's active duty service and lived on a base together for one year, but that was long enough for me to experience the chaos and the excitement of being a military wife.

At the age of 28, I was newly married and expecting our first child. My husband and I were living apart so that I could be closer to family. I had an extended hospital stay due to bacterial pneumonia early in my pregnancy and needed to rely on help from my parents while Joe's squadron was traveling between Lemoore, California, and Fallon, Nevada. Joe lived in the barracks on base at Lemoore. I lived and worked in Phoenix, Arizona. He was a jet engine mechanic on the F-18 and two years earlier had severely injured his back while working. He was finally scheduled to have surgery at Naval Medical Center, San Diego, when I was 38 weeks pregnant. Our plan was for him to have the operation, recover in the hospital for a few days, and then spend his 45 days of convalescent leave in Phoenix with me while we waited for the birth of our daughter.

It sounded like a good plan.

In the wee hours of May 2, 2005, I said goodnight to my husband on the phone and wished him all the best before his surgery the next day. Several hours later my water broke, but I didn't realize what happened. I thought I was just so huge that I'd had an accident. I fell back asleep and the next morning began my usual routine. I waited for the phone notification that Joe was out of surgery. As the day wore on I noticed that something was not right. I was leaking fluid, but I thought it was because the baby was pressing against my bladder. I called my doctor's office and the nurse said that it was most likely amniotic fluid that was slowly trickling out. I went to the hospital, and since I did not have any contractions I was given

Pitocin to start my labor. As soon as my groggy husband called to say he was in recovery, I told him my water broke. He nervously reassured me that everything would be okay, and he would be there to see the birth because he was determined to leave the hospital! We had done everything we could so that his surgery would be scheduled close to my due date, but with enough time for him to somewhat recover. I was panicked and heartbroken that he would not be with me for the birth. His hospital stay was expected to be three days.

My dad lived close by. He gathered my bags and prepared to drive me to the hospital when Joe called again. He said he convinced his medical team to let him leave the hospital. He was bound and determined to be there for the birth. The neurosurgeon was not pleased, but signed the release paperwork. Still in a wheelchair, Joe was dropped off curbside by my mother-in-law at the San Diego airport where he caught a commercial flight to Arizona. Two hours before our baby was born, Joe wheeled into the delivery room still wearing the wrist bands from the Navy hospital. Surprisingly, he was not in pain—a condition we later attributed to a combination of adrenaline and pain medication. Soon after midnight we welcomed Mary Grace into the wild world of Navy baby-hood. I was overjoyed that she was here and that my husband and I experienced that moment together.

In the following days, we adjusted to becoming a family. Each night brought the painful reminder of how short 45 days of convalescent leave really was. Joe would soon have to report back to the base in California, and I would be alone with a newborn. We were on the waiting list for base housing, but who knew how long that would take?

Unfortunately, two weeks later Joe had discoloration and swelling at the incision site. He tried unsuccessfully to contact his doctor in San Diego, so my dad took him to the VA Hospital emergency room. Joe's surgical site had become infected. Two days later we drove to San Diego in the summer heat with our two-week old baby, who was not even old enough for vaccinations, to a military hospital where deployed sailors and Marines were continually returning and bringing all of those overseas germs home.

Joe ended up staying in the hospital for almost a month and had three more operations. I stayed with friends or in Joe's hospital room. I was in an unfamiliar city and struggled to tend to him, our baby, and myself. I cried myself to sleep every night and thought about how unfair my first month of motherhood was. I had envisioned our happy family at home relaxing and introducing loved ones to our new bundle of joy. I was tired of being in a hospital and trying to nurse my baby in a waiting room full of sailors. I was also very scared that Joe wouldn't live. He had spinal fluid leaks that were difficult to repair. He had also re-herniated the disks that were initially operated on, something the doctor said was common in larger stature men like Joe. At 6'4 and 225 pounds, he was difficult to even position correctly on the operating table, according to the surgeons.

Early on a Sunday morning when Joe was going to have his fourth operation, I held my baby as I sat in a stiff plastic chair and stared blankly at the floor. A neurosurgeon put his hand on my arm and said, "I know this is hard and it seems like it will never end, but all of you will get through this. I'm going to stop this leak and a year from now, this entire experience will seem like a bad dream."

After a four-hour operation, the doctor returned to the waiting room to tell me of the successful surgery. I was eternally thankful for my husband's life and for the chance to move on and enjoy our little family. Not long after that, we returned to Arizona for the relaxation I had been craving. After three months of convalescent leave, Joe had to return to Lemoore. Within two months we moved into base housing and it was almost like we were never apart.

Two years later, I look back at that nightmare and realize how much we learned from it. We gained new strength in our marriage, confidence as parents, and a deeper respect for Navy medicine. Since then I've helped my husband through his recovery and the Physical Evaluation Board process where he was granted a medical retirement. He is a full-time student and looks forward to a new career he can be equally passionate about. My husband and I will always look back on the Navy experience with a sense of accomplishment and pride.

DEBORAH LOGAN HORSTKOTTE enjoys volunteering and being active in her community in the San Diego area. Along with caring for two high-functioning special needs daughters and a husband who was injured on active duty, she's an advocate for military caregivers and special education. In 2016, she received the Mattie J.T. Stepanek award for military caregivers from former First Lady Rosalynn Carter.

My Brilliant Life Plan
Phyllis Denton

In 1965 we'd been living well and having a grand time at
Ernest Harmon AFB in Newfoundland, Canada. Harmon was
located in the southwest corner of the island of Newfoundland.
In those days most aircraft, civilian and military, couldn't carry
enough fuel to fly from the U.S. to Europe. Newfoundland
was the final refueling outpost before heading across the North
Atlantic. Besides serving as a ground fuel depot, there was also
an air refueling squadron of KC-97s based there. My husband
was a pilot of one of those "flying gas stations."

Harmon was considered to be an isolated location, and it
was. But the Air Force compensated for the assignment by
providing excellent facilities for the personnel and their families. The base housing was good, there was a full service
hospital and dental clinic, schools, library, chapel, gymnasium,
parks and picnic grounds, and every sort of fully equipped
hobby and craft shop our small community could possibly
need. If they didn't have it, they would get it. There were
always lots of parties and activities to keep us occupied. And
there was also lots of snow—12 feet a year! We used to giggle
about schlepping across the parking lot to a party wearing
knee boots, ski jackets, and long gowns—skirts hoisted up and
strappy sandals in hand. There was a Currier-and-Ives-worthy
site on base with a long hill for sledding and tobogganing and
a pond at the bottom for skating. Ice skating was always a community effort. Since it hardly ever stopped snowing in the
winter, the pond always had to be cleared before anyone could
skate. No Zamboni there—just lots of daddies with snow
shovels. A few of the men on base had ingeniously rigged up a
rope tow for the skiers. It was all great family fun. In the
summer, the snow finally went away and the most beautiful
flowers I've ever seen burst into life.

Besides all the amenities, household help was available
and affordable from the genial Newfoundlanders in nearby

Stephenville. A young woman named Mary lived with us during the week to help with housekeeping, laundry, and child care. She went home on weekends but was available for babysitting in the evenings if we needed her. Life was fun, life was good, life was easy. Best of all, it was a sure-fire, cast-in-stone, guaranteed three-year tour of duty, which could even be extended to six years if requested. That guarantee was what prompted the revision of our grand life plan: Why not have our fourth baby there?

We had moved to Newfoundland in February 1965 and our third child was born shortly afterwards in May. Two or three months after she was born, I got to thinking: we were planning to have a fourth child in a couple of years anyway. Why not move the family planning calendar up a year? That way I could have the extra household help with the children that I needed but couldn't afford in the U.S., and we knew for certain that I wouldn't have to face a move when I was either pregnant or toting a newborn. It was a well-established maxim among Air Force wives that a move would occur either just before or just after a new baby. Not this time! I calculated by the time we moved again, our family would be complete and the youngest would be at least two years old—maybe even five if we extended our tour there. Yes! I got absolutely lightheaded with the brilliance of my plan.

So I stopped nursing the three-month old baby and started ovulating. Very shortly after that it became clear to me I must be pregnant again, a condition that happened much more quickly than I anticipated. My doctor confirmed it with a lab test. The brilliant life plan was in motion!

One week later, the Air Force announced Harmon AFB was closing permanently and everyone stationed there would move within the year.

The news was more devastating than anything I could've imagined. I was pregnant and soon we would have four kids under the age of five, but we wouldn't be at Harmon AFB, where life was easy and fun, where I had domestic help and the kids had lots of open space and plenty of other children to play with. Who knew where we would end up? This was the worst news ever!

But orders are orders, so six months later on a spring day in May we left Harmon in a raging blizzard, our intrepid VW bus loaded to the gunwales, and headed for the port at Port aux Basques. We had booked passage on the *M.V. William Carson*, a famous ice-breaking ferry that traversed the Cabot Strait between Port aux Basques, Newfoundland and North Sydney, Nova Scotia. The departure of the *Willie Carson* was delayed four hours that day due to high winds and high seas. All things considered, that day—May 8, 1966—seemed an ominous glimpse into our next Air Force adventure.

I had insisted on reserving a cabin on the ferry for our comfort and convenience, especially my own. My husband had objected, saying it was too expensive. Easy for him to say; he wasn't the one with the big belly and three clingy preschoolers. He agreed my idea was a good one after all, once I explained my alternative plan: that I would meet up with him and his children at the airport in Bangor, Maine. It was a very good thing we did have a cabin that day. The kids and I had a terrific time wandering about the ship; the father unit was so seasick he was literally green and didn't emerge from *my* cabin once during the eight hour trip. (About ten years later the *M.V. William Carson* tragically hit an iceberg and sank.)

And so, come hell *and* high water, we began our three-week journey from Newfoundland to Oklahoma—half a continent and worlds away.

It was on this trip, when we were eating all our meals in restaurants, that I became acutely aware that all three of our knee-high munchkins had acquired quite a taste for lobster, the kind we were able to buy by the boxful for 50 cents apiece from the fishermen on the beach in Newfoundland. Back in the real world, lobster for a three-year-old was extravagant. Luckily, none of them could read, so we just told them lobster wasn't on the menu. How about a corn dog instead? Besides, as any parent who has taken a family road trip can tell you, kids can survive for weeks on French fries.

Our grand adventure out of Newfoundland started with a two-month temporary duty at Tinker AFB, Oklahoma, between "permanent" assignments. We had to set up camp in a cramped, two-bedroom, furnished apartment that any reasonable person would deem sub-standard. The wonder of it was that we could find a place to live at all. Fortunately, we had no pets at the time, but we did have three, soon to be four, small children, and we were only going to live there for 60 days—not exactly the sort of tenant most property owners hope for. Fortunately, Tinker had a long history as a training base so the locals were set up to handle the transient traffic. There were many large, privately-owned, furnished apartment complexes to support the mission at Tinker. There was also a swimming pool and wall-to-wall kids of all sizes who did a fine job of keeping each other happy and busy at play.

The apartment had an air conditioner, a solitary window unit in the wee living room that didn't begin to meet the needs of the day or the night. Our vehicle of choice that summer was the aforementioned VW bus, also not air conditioned. The temperature never once went below 90 degrees, day or night, for the entire time we lived there. Coping with the heat was the hardest part of that summer for me. At the time I could not fathom how anyone could stand to live in Oklahoma, or why they'd want to. (We were assigned to Oklahoma bases two more times in subsequent years, and I learned to love it and to cope with the heat. It just took practice.)

One hot day halfway through our stay, I went to the base hospital and gave birth to our fourth daughter. At under five pounds, her birth weight was "below minimums," so she stayed in the hospital a few days longer than I did. Since 1966 pre-dated the invention of a breast pump that actually worked, every three hours I headed down the highway to the base hospital in my VW bus to nurse my newborn. But first, every three hours I had to shower and change into clean clothes because I was so sweaty from the heat. My other children, ages one, three, and five were usually cared for by my many wonderful newfound friends and neighbors and their teenage children—military families all—living in the apartment complex.

With four healthy daughters, I had much to be grateful for. Still, I had a list of gripes and miseries as long as my arm—

and growing. I hadn't bargained for the six of us camping out in a cramped apartment in a place as hot as Hades! It was hard to believe just a year earlier I had hatched the most brilliant scheme ever for a smooth family life, or as smooth as Air Force family life could be. But poor planning, or even no planning, would have resulted in a more satisfactory outcome. You know the old adage, "Life is what happens while you're planning something else"? I had been planning something else.

PHYLLIS DENTON is proud to say that of her five daughters, four are married to the military and three of them were active duty members themselves. She now lives in Las Cruces, New Mexico, where she often plays host to visiting family, which now includes 11 grandchildren.

Michael's Story
LISA GLEN

"Yes, I'll get a roommate!" shouted Gabriel, age four, as he pumped both fists high into the air. The only boy in our family of six children was finally going to have a brother!

Thus began our journey with a baby boy due in four months. Fast forward three months to May 26, 2006, our 21st wedding anniversary! Baby, as yet unnamed, wasn't due for another three weeks. I had some contractions that morning, but none of my children arrived earlier than their due date, so I wasn't concerned. The six kids and I walked the mile to the West Point Parade Field for the Class of 2006 graduation parade. My husband, Andy, met us there and I let him know I thought today might be the day, since the contractions were growing stronger and closer together on our walk. During the parade, the contractions got more intense! When the First Captain shouted, "Pass in Review," I told Andy, "It's time!" He didn't take me seriously, so I emphasized that we had to go, NOW!

There was one minor problem: our car was on the other side of the parade field and no traffic was allowed in the vicinity. Our parish priest was standing near us and quickly figured out a solution. He told the Military Police that we needed to get to the hospital. A friend took our six kids while Andy and I left. Fortunately, a maintenance vehicle in the area drove us the mile to Keller Army Hospital.

Andy still didn't think this was it, but I certainly knew! Because I had a history of quick and easy (but not painless!) deliveries, the nurses asked if they could deliver the baby. We had no problem with that and were happy to let them share in our joy. Our biggest concern was that we still didn't agree on a name for the little guy. He was born less than an hour after our arrival at the hospital, and the rest of the family came by to meet him shortly thereafter. All was well with our newly expanded family of nine.

Since we still didn't have a name picked out, the nurses started calling the baby "George W," in honor of the guest speaker at West Point's graduation. That evening, Baby Boy was having problems maintaining his temperature. He also didn't latch on when nursing and kept having variations in his blood sugar levels.

Nothing seemed too unusual to us until the doctor said the next morning that the baby needed to be transferred by air to the nearby children's hospital for evaluation and care. This was West Point's graduation day and, as it turned out, the aircraft was not allowed to come to the hospital since the president was on post. (Note: I'm sure if it were a life-or-death situation, the clearance would have been granted.) We followed the ambulance to the Maria Fareri Children's Hospital in Westchester, New York, glibly thinking the baby would be evaluated and released the next day. Little did we know that the hospital would be our home-away-from-home for the next eight months.

Meanwhile, our community back home shifted into emergency mode. My sister Maria had unexpectedly come from Cape Cod to see the baby and ended up staying at the house for several days. She dealt with all the daily activities: cooking, cleaning, laundry, carpooling, and then was hit with the unexpected! All six kids got the stomach flu and not many made it to the bathroom on the first try!

Once Maria returned home to her own family, our Most Holy Trinity church family, the U.S. Military Academy Math Department family, Sacred Heart of Jesus School family, and neighbors started cooking meals, watching kids, cleaning house, doing laundry, and basically taking over parenting duties under the close scrutiny of our wonderfully competent 14-year-old daughter, Andrea.

At the hospital we were bluntly informed that our baby probably had Down Syndrome but we wouldn't know for sure until chromosomal testing came back in two weeks. We also found out he had a congenital heart defect and that he would need open heart surgery. Truthfully, the news of the heart defect and other medical concerns hit us the hardest. We were completely prepared to deal with the Down Syndrome and the special needs of a child (we have another "special" child with autism). At that point God gave us a supernatural sense of peace about the whole situation which prevails today.

After much prayer and reading Saints' biographies, we picked out the name Michael Anthony. We knew that with the name of an Archangel *and* a Franciscan, this little guy would be blanketed with God's grace.

After being off medication for a week, Michael got to come home, with the doctor's admonition to "watch him and bring him in if he gets worse!" How scary is that? Less than six weeks later we noticed some heavy, labored breathing so we took him to the hospital. Diagnosed with congestive heart failure, he was admitted for what would be the second of six inpatient stints at the children's hospital.

The community and our families again jumped into action and took over our household and children duties so Andy and I could stay at the hospital. It was such a relief to stay by Michael's side knowing our Army family was taking care of the home front. We were also fortunate to get into "Ronald's House," a Ronald McDonald Family Room one floor up from the Pediatric ICU. The ability to take turns sleeping, resting, and spending a few minutes away from the hospital environment was refreshing, especially since we could do it just one minute from our baby's side. Michael had two more stays at the hospital with high fevers and breathing difficulties. We thought by his two-month birthday that everything was holding steady, and we were preparing for open heart surgery when he turned four months. He ended up back in the hospital with broken ribs resulting from a severe Vitamin D deficiency and osteopenia (very brittle bones). Michael also kept having high "fevers of unknown origin" which are common in kids with Down Syndrome.

On July 27, at two months and one day old, Michael's fever spiked to 106.5 degrees (and most likely higher). I was up all night with the nurses and residents trying to get it down with medication, cool water, and ice packs. The fever kept building and Michael's breathing was erratic and labored. At 5:30 a.m., after an incredibly long night of action and prayer, I had one of what I've named an "inspired by the Holy Spirit" moment and called Andy, who had gone home to visit the kids.

"Come back to the hospital right away!" I said. When Andy arrived, the charge nurse went to the Pediatric ICU and brought back an intensive care doctor. He took one look at Michael and pulled the crib out of the room. "Let's go!" he shouted. In the elevator on the way to the ICU, Michael's heart and breathing stopped—he went into cardiac and respiratory arrest. (At first Andy and I were relieved, thinking Michael was finally getting some sleep. We had a rude awakening.) Dr. Singh "bagged" him with oxygen and a few seconds later when we arrived in the ICU we heard the worst phrase I had ever heard in my life: "Start CPR." The team of 16 began CPR and lifesaving measures. Within a few minutes, Michael was back with us—what a relief! The doctor said, "Naughty boy, Michael! Please don't do that again!" which broke the tension in the room. Within the span of a few minutes we had experienced the worst and best day of our life. We both remarked later that this lifesaving effort was very much like a military operation. Each person had a role and an intern talked us through the entire scenario.

Michael wasn't quite out of the woods. After his brush with mortality, he ended up with pneumonia, more broken ribs, a perforated bowel (which was his second near-death experience), ostomy surgery, Pulmonary Artery Banding surgery (a closed heart procedure) and more. The goal was to get him healthy enough to make it to his open heart surgery. Over the next seven weeks he was heavily sedated and on the respirator. We started a web page at a site called Carepages.com which allowed us to post daily updates, photographs, and receive e-mail from all those who were praying for us and encouraging us. This was a lifesaver because it allowed me to journal the ongoing events and let people know what specific prayers were needed.

After this long hospitalization, Michael came home to heal and grow. He had ostomy reversal surgery in November 2006—we were never so happy to see a poopy diaper! He had open heart surgery in January 2007 and is healing well. His brother and sisters love him dearly and are the best therapists Michael will ever have. He has an incredible army of therapists, nurses, and doctors on his team who don't just take care of his medical and developmental needs, they *love* him. This little fighter is a unifier, whose daily struggles and victories have been prayed for by more than three hundred website subscribers and their families around the world: family and friends from our West Point cadet days, 30 years in the Army, church communities, Keller Hospital, Maria Fareri Hospital, and all over. We see each day a physical manifestation of all of those prayers in precious Michael Anthony Glen.

Post Script, 2019: Michael is now an active, healthy 12-year-old who is beloved by family and friends. He is in sixth grade at our neighborhood school and is in a fully inclusive environment with the curriculum adapted to his needs. He enjoys playing with friends, jumping on the trampoline, hiking, watching music videos and movies, and playing jokes on all of us!

LISA GLEN and Andy have been married 34 years and are blessed with eight beautiful children (with the addition of Claire in 2010)—two with special needs and all special in their own way! Lisa is a full-time mom and retired Army Aviator with 13 years active service and eight years in the Army Reserves. Andy retired in 2014 after 30 years of active duty service, and the family moved to their forever home in Colorado. Lisa volunteers at the children's schools, at church, and in the community, and Andy continues teaching as an adjunct professor at a local college.

It's in the Water
KELLY PIKE

Jeff and I had just married and he was beginning his Army career. We were sent off to a dream location, Hawaii, for our first assignment. The ideas of the perfect marriage were really becoming a reality. We would live by the ocean, picnic on the beach for dinner, and walk barefoot in the sand listening to the waves at dusk. What a life!

This was, of course, also the perfect time to start a family. We were settled in, Jeff was happy at work, and I was making friends with other Army spouses. Because many were parents, the talk those days centered on children. The joke when we arrived was "something's in the water," as in, don't drink it if you don't want to be pregnant. Needless to say, I drank plenty of water, but never got pregnant.

Anxious, off to the doctor I went. First stop, Family Practice. I was interviewed, examined and had blood taken. The doctor determined I was healthy, just needed a little thyroid medication and some time. He said, "Take your basal body temperature every day and fill out these charts." Waiting was not my specialty (still isn't), but I was young and could still give it time. Meanwhile, Karen, Debbie, Beth, Marie, and Kathy all became pregnant from the water, and I was excited for them, but crushed on the inside. Was my water coming from a different well?

Even after we left Hawaii, we had similar experiences, but by now we had gotten a few years older, knew my basal body temperature by heart, and were even more frustrated. The Army hospitals didn't have much in the way of infertility treatment, and by the way, I had to go to the Obstetrics clinic for treatment! Had they lost their minds? After five years of trying to have children, I was asked to sit in the OB clinic and hear all the women complain about their pregnancies, while I tried to be cheerful about not being pregnant. Overhearing stories of "accidents" and "not a good time to be pregnant" saddened my heart beyond belief and made it nearly impossible to hold back tears.

After another move, we were referred to Brooks Army Medical Center in San Antonio for infertility treatment. They actually had their own clinic and doctors who specialized in this area. Of course, they were also training other doctors, so every appointment I felt more and more like a lab rat; I was poked, prodded, and examined by a panel of doctors with even more doctors watching! The phrase "just relax" became a joke as I was laying spread eagle for all to see. It would be worth it in the end, I thought, if I could just get pregnant.

Many of my friends became obsessed with giving me great advice on getting pregnant. "Have you tried standing on your head for thirty minutes after sex?" Or "Try propping up on pillows." Or "Just relax, (oh, how I began to despise that word) and it will happen." Or the really well-meaning, but quite flippant, "You can have mine" remark! Probably the most hurtful comment of all was, "Why don't you just adopt?" Just adopt? Did they think I wanted a puppy? Did they have the $25,000 it would take to adopt a child? Did they just not get it? I wanted to be pregnant! I wanted to experience the whole process!

The next move took us to New York and more possibilities. We were off to Bethesda Naval Hospital for more "treatment" with more specially-trained doctors. My diagnosis now changed from "You're young, give it time" to "Your ovaries are responding to this medication as if they were over 40!" At the time I was in my early 30s, well short of that magic cut-off. I continued trying fertility meds, in-vitro, in-vitro with a few twists, and gathering more advice. My new friends were having babies, but going to their showers became impossible for me. After listening to delivery story after story, and those "It's in the water" comments, I couldn't muster the smile or hide the tears long enough to attend, so I began sending my gifts with friends.

The infertility experience was such a roller coaster of emotions. Trying new procedures, taking my temperature before moving each morning, having Jeff administer shots in my hip three times a day, drinking the water, waiting to see if the procedure worked, taking my temperature some more, listening to more advice, getting more fertility drugs, waiting to see if the procedure worked. Would I ever get pregnant?

Even after 14 years of treatments, I never did get to experience being pregnant. I was frustrated and exhausted from all the ups and downs of dreams made and crushed emotionally. It was then that God brought several couples with adopted children into our lives. We could clearly see their joy. As we heard their stories, we felt excitement and hope that a possible end to our roller coaster ride was near.

After much discussion and prayer, we decided to adopt. Jeff and I traveled to Russia first, and then a year and a half later, to Kazakhstan, to bring home two beautiful boys who will keep us young well into our "older" age. I have to admit, the minute they were placed in our arms, we couldn't have been more ecstatic or loved them any more had I actually given birth to them. The costs, emotional and monetary, were just a drop in the bucket compared to our joy as parents. They are ours and we are theirs. Together we are forever a family.

By the way, where they came from, we were told NOT to drink the water!

KELLY PIKE lives in Louisiana with her husband of 32 years, Jeff, and her two boys, Matthew and Michael, who are students at Louisiana Tech University. She enjoys teaching computer classes to middle school students, living in the country, and spending time with family.

Special Delivery at Gate Five
MARY BETH SMITH

Gate Five at the Savannah/Hilton Head International Airport will always be one of my favorite places. On the morning of July 13, 2005, my newborn son and I made our way through the security checkpoint after obtaining our special pass. We decorated the stroller with "Welcome Home" signs, made sure the camera was ready and anxiously awaited the next incoming flight. My husband Jeremy was on that flight returning to Fort Stewart for his two weeks of mid-tour leave during Operation Iraqi Freedom III as part of the Army's 3rd Infantry Division. It would be the first time he'd see his newborn son in person.

Eight weeks earlier, our first child, Parker, arrived at the Winn Army Community Hospital while I was on the phone with my husband. Due to some minor pregnancy complications, the doctor had scheduled an induction for a Monday morning. While nervous about the induction, it was a logistical blessing. Jeremy was able to arrange to borrow the unit chaplain's satellite phone and knew when my mother and I were headed to labor and delivery. He checked in every couple of hours throughout the labor. Late in the evening at Fort Stewart and early the next morning in Iraq, he dialed the hospital and the nursing staff estimated that he should call back in half an hour when it would be just about time to meet the little guy. Unfortunately, the doctor walked in the room about five minutes later and decided it would be just fine to have the baby right then! Through God's grace, the phone rang again just a few minutes later and Jeremy stayed on the phone for the delivery. My mom devoted most of her attention to the nursing staff and me but managed to keep talking to Jeremy so he had some idea of what was happening. Immediately after Parker arrived, I took the phone and talked to Jeremy for a couple of minutes reassuring him that we were all doing well. Thankfully, it was a cloudless night and the satellite phone did not disconnect us even once.

It was unbelievable to us that when our first child arrived, Jeremy was sitting half a world away, looking at a million stars in the sky outside of his trailer, on a different calendar day of the year. Yet, he was there with us. We were so happy that we had a safe delivery of a healthy baby, and that we had shared it together. The very thoughtful battalion commander's wife rushed over to the hospital for a quick visit to take pictures of our new son so Jeremy could see him via emailed photos within a few hours. The proud dad made sure the announcement was published in the *Taji Times*, the newspaper at Camp Taji where he was stationed. The new dad also had a big box of treats for his soldiers: bubble gum cigars, new baby mints, and lots of office decorations and banners.

The joy (and adrenaline) didn't fully wear off until Parker and I arrived back home two days later. Within a few moments of walking in the door of our home, I sat down on the couch with our tiny baby and our little dog and the realities of the lonely days ahead started to cover the stars with clouds. The idea of parenting alone during a deployment was a tough concept, especially to someone who had changed her first diaper less than 48 hours ago! Now that the security of that satellite phone was gone, how were we going to share this experience of parenting our son? I was anxious, exhausted, and determined to rise to the challenge. Fortunately, we had already laid a good foundation of communication, so I built on that.

Jeremy deployed when I was 22 weeks and one day into the pregnancy. Given that I was lucky not to have early pregnancy sickness, he was essentially there for the good part.

What did expecting our first child mean to us in the face of a year-long deployment? It meant finding out the baby's sex was a given. Every bit of information we could share was a bonus; we happily watched the ultrasound video together and learned we would have a son. It meant that we put together nursery furniture in month four instead of month eight. It meant that we strategically placed pictures of Jeremy throughout the nursery and taped him reading books so the little guy would recognize his voice. It meant that my husband arranged to have flowers delivered every month on our anniversary date (which turned out to be the baby's birth date in Iraq). Thus, I have pregnancy belly photos next to a bouquet of flowers on the seventeenth of every month for the last two trimesters. It meant that we made the tough decision to request the R&R leave for a couple of months after the baby's arrival. It meant that every gift that arrived was photographed wrapped *and* unwrapped and listed in a letter. It meant that phone calls from Iraq in the middle of the night were no big deal since odds were good that I was awake. It meant that my husband really thought about what he wanted his child to know about life, and he put those thoughts on paper.

Following Parker's arrival, I was blessed to have my mom's help for a few weeks. To include my husband in the early baby days, we tried to document as much as we could, just as I had done during the final weeks of the pregnancy. I wrote letters and mailed something every day there was postal service that year. It was tiring to write down all the minutia of life with baby, but I felt the love was in the details and Jeremy deserved to know all of it. I took digital photos nearly every day which resulted in a three-volume baby book!

It may seem unusual to be so happy about an airport memory. After all, we didn't get to have the "magic bonding hour" after the baby's arrival as a new little family. Daddy didn't videotape the baby's homecoming or first bath or even his first Christmas when he was seven months old. But Gate Five at the Savannah/Hilton Head International Airport will always be special to Jeremy, Parker, and me since it was the first place we all got to be together as a family. When Jeremy finally walked through the jet way, he had a huge smile on his face. He spotted us right away and within seconds had little Parker in his arms. Parker stared in awe at his daddy's face as if to say, "I think I know you" and offered his baby grin. The joy of those first moments is just as valid as if we had shared them in the delivery room. The passengers waiting to board the outgoing flight also shared the joy as it was obvious that this new Dad in his Desert Combat Uniform was meeting the tiny baby in his red, white, and blue outfit for the first time. They smiled and offered to take pictures of our little family and one sweet elderly lady told me it had just made her day to watch my husband come off of that airplane and see that little baby.

While the two weeks of leave went by too quickly, there was still enough time for baby's baptism, first baseball game, first splash in a pool, and first reminder to "Beat Navy" after the bedtime prayers were said.

I have another unusual favorite place in the Fort Stewart area. It's called Cottrell Gym. Due to weather issues, it was where the homecoming ceremony took place for Jeremy's return at the end of the yearlong deployment. The roar of the crowd when the first soldier stepped over the threshold of that gym is a sound I will never forget. For Parker and me, seeing our soldier home for more than just a visit was incredible.

We were ready for a new beginning as a family. A family of three. And nine months later, a family of four.

MARY BETH SMITH transitioned from Air Force brat to Army wife in 2000. She has a BS in International Management from Butler University and is a recipient of the Catherine Greene Award for Outstanding Volunteerism from the Association of Quartermasters. Her interests include exploring surrounding communities at each Army post, running road races, playing the piano, reading, and scrapbooking. She resides in Burke, Virginia, with her husband and three sons.

Friends, Family, and Everything in Between

Flying Solo
MARTHA MERRITT

I have flashes of panic after I leave my husband at some middle-of-the-night, better-have-all-your-gear-and-be-prepared-to-say-goodbye-for-"x"-number-of-weeks drop-off point. I always think the worst: that we've overlooked something, that I'll need his signature or his advice, that he left a small but important item, like his beret, laying on the living room couch.

I don't know why I panic. That's what Army packing lists are for. That's why he and I sit down a couple days beforehand and get bills and time-sensitive correspondence done. That's why I have a power-of-attorney. And thus far, the only thing I see that he forgot is the bag of cookies I made for him to take along. If that's all he's forgotten, we're in good shape.

After leaving my husband at Fort Riley at 2 a.m., I drove 30 minutes home, which gave me time to consider this life. When I got back to my kitchen, I started putting my thoughts down on paper.

Who else knowingly, willingly, and supportively sends her spouse to "work" for weeks or months at a time? Who else doesn't cry or whine or pout because in comparison to the last training exercise at Fort Irwin, three and a half weeks is nothing? Who else eats dinners on the couch rather than sitting at the kitchen table alone? Or sleeps alone in a queen-sized bed with a row of pillows on the other side? Or takes care of cutting the lawn and taking out the garbage because there isn't the choice to wait for the man to do it?

The women who proudly answered, "Me!" to these questions are the members who make up this unique life. This life often strikes me with awe and an overwhelming sense of pride, knowing that I am a part of such an exceptional community.

The threads of this community weave us tightly together, when in the "real" world, our paths probably wouldn't even cross. I've befriended, confided in, and trusted women with whom, at first glance, I had little in common, except an indefinable sense of sisterhood knowing they'd lived through the same struggles, triumphs, heartaches, and joys as I had. Like Danielle. She was younger, more Southern, and more outgoing than I'll ever be, but she was also able to understand my feelings as if she were my sister.

There is something about this community that makes me feel automatically drawn to another person with an out-of-state license plate or the unmistakable DOD sticker on the windshield. There is something that makes me reach out to them even if the person is someone I wouldn't have considered approaching before. Philosophical and lifestyle differences that previously would have been deal-breakers are suddenly put into new perspective. I realize that friendship has less to do with finding a person who *is* just like me and more to do with finding a person who *feels* just like me.

I am an Army wife, living in Kansas. I'm used to having my husband gone, used to him crawling home at night late, tired and dirty, used to a life of IDs and stickers, and constant accountability, from morning formations to mandatory leave forms. This is home.

I've been sitting here writing long enough that it is now close to 5 a.m., and our dark little subdivision is starting to stir, two hours before the rest of the town. Just another reflection of how this life runs on a schedule separate from the civilian world. The members of this unofficial military community have started quietly backing out of their driveways and heading southwest to Fort Riley for another day of *our* life.

MARTHA MERRITT is a proud Army wife who lives with her husband, Clinton, near Fort Riley, Kansas. She teaches high school English and enjoys writing in her free time.

Wanted: New Best Friend
WENDY BARRETT

Thirty-something mother of four seeks friend experienced in deployments, TDYs, and pre-algebra. Potty training and band concert experience a plus. Requirements include window shopping, brownie taste testing, and a flexible schedule.

As we prepared to move from Rapid City, South Dakota, to Hawaii where my husband would be the only Air Force officer in an Army brigade, I worried! I worried about shipping our car. I worried about our middle schooler leaving her two best friends. I worried about our kindergartener going from half-day to full-day school. I worried about being the only Air Force family on an Army base (whoops! I mean Army *post*. I always get that wrong!) I worried about my husband's job change, and the movers, and our lovely leather couches making it across the ocean safely.

With all my to-do lists and worrying, I forgot about me. I didn't ask myself "Would I be okay? Would I make friends? Would I be happy?" I just didn't have time.

After a few weeks, everything I was initially worried about worked itself out. Eating lunch at school was an adventure for our kindergartener. My husband was thriving in his new job and even seemed to be enjoying the physical training. Our household goods arrived mostly safe and sound, and the kids were settling into school and making friends in the neighborhood.

And I was lonely.

I had to remind myself that sometimes it just takes time to find a best buddy. So I gave myself the same pep-talk I gave my seventh grader: smile, say "Hi," don't put-down others, find a way to be a friend, and don't worry about being different.

Finding *that* friend after a move with the military is both challenging and crucial. We military wives need friends. Even the most self-sufficient of us needs someone to lean on when times get tough.

We need support for ourselves when our husbands are deployed. We are not geographically close to family so our friends often take on that role in times of need and celebration. Those friends will see us on our bad hair days and in our good moments. They'll be emergency contacts for our kids and join us for cake and ice cream at birthday parties. Friends who'll understand the rhythms of a military family and know I'm not available for babysitting or pedicures for the first couple weeks after my husband returns home.

But finding *that* friend quickly is crucial because we're working against a deadline. Only three years at this duty station, and for me, just seven months until my husband heads away to Iraq. A good friend makes all the difference during a deployment. But finding *that* friend can be hard.

It's been six months since the move. Not our first move. Maybe our sixth move in seven years? I'm not sure. All of this moving takes a toll on our furniture as well as our friendships. I've discovered that finding a friend is sometimes harder than getting the finance office to update your cost-of-living-allowance, but so much more rewarding.

Last week we were at the beach with another family. The kids were all playing comfortably in the sand. I grabbed a boogie board and raced out to ride some waves with my friend, Diane.

And it hit me: Diane was that friend. A real friend, the kind who'll call in the middle of the night if she goes into labor before her mom gets into town. The kind who'll bring me chocolate ice cream when my husband deploys. The kind I will hate to leave in a few years when the time comes. For now, though, we're watching for the next good wave and I'm not worrying about a thing.

WENDY BARRETT lives in Hawaii with her husband and four children. She enjoys eating pineapple, scuba diving, and falling off her surfboard. You can read all about her laundry, to-do lists, and adventures as an Air Force wife at www.rapidlife.blogspot.com.

Becoming Family
DEVIN PATTON

I will never forget the day my husband came home from his Human Resources job and "asked" me if he could join the Army. It was the middle of 2005, and we had been a nation at war for over two years. Dissent for the war was really beginning to peak, and he wanted to show his support for the country. He just had lunch with SSG Mayberry, a recruiter out of Fort Sam Houston, Texas. After a lengthy conversation, a lot of questions, and a few tears, I called the sergeant and invited him to our home for dinner so I could find out more about the Army. He came over the very next evening.

I grew up next to Camp Pendleton Marine Base in southern California and had heard stories about promises made by recruiters and not kept. While I was completely supportive of the military and their mission, I was extremely wary of military recruiters. In retrospect I went into the conversation with the mindset that I would take everything he said with a grain of salt. Little did I know I was about to meet a man who lived his life according to the Seven Core Values, including Integrity. SSG Mayberry pulled no punches as he told us of the chances of my husband deploying to a war zone and of the expectations we'd have to live up to as members of the military. When I say "members" I mean that he explained I would be a military spouse and part of the military family. That meant if I got a speeding ticket, my husband's chain of command would hear about it. It also meant that I would become part of a network of wives and families who would support me in times of need and be there to share in our family's accomplishments and growth.

My husband graduated from Basic Training and Advanced Individual Training with honors in June 2006 and was assigned to Fort Lee, Virginia. I arrived with plans of being the perfect Army wife. I had it all figured out. I would make friends with all the other wives and volunteer for the Family Readiness

Group. I baked cookies for the first sergeant's birthday. I volunteered to help with the Christmas party and let the commander know I was available to help out in any way I could. But it seemed they didn't need my help. I didn't feel welcome at the meetings, and no one took me up on my offers to help out with parties and barbecues.

In January 2007, when my husband deployed to Iraq, I felt very alone. His friends I knew deployed too. We were still on the waiting list for housing, so I learned how to use a gun; I felt unsafe in my neighborhood. I decided I was going to use my husband's deployment as an opportunity to prove that I could really be on my own. I could pay the bills, fix flat tires, fight off large raccoons, handle sewage backups, and mow the lawn. I could do this!

Then our TV broke. I needed it to stay informed on Iraq, so I went to the PX and bought a new one. They loaded it in my car. I brought it home and got my neighbor to bring it in the house. Then I realized it wasn't going to fit in our entertainment center because TVs aren't square anymore—they're wide. So I went to Wal-Mart and bought a stand and put it together myself. By this time it was 9 p.m. and I couldn't go knocking on my neighbor's door, so I decided I could lift the TV on the stand myself. Our old entertainment center was huge but I wedged myself between it and the wall and used my legs to slowly inch it out of the way to make room for the new stand. Once I did that, I only had to lift the TV a foot and a half off the ground. After I dropped and dented my new TV and bruised my legs (I thought I would use them to protect the TV when I dropped it), I realized I couldn't do it. The next day I called the one soldier I knew who hadn't deployed and asked him to put my TV on the stand, which he did, for a *fee*. I hooked up the cable and the surround sound and felt very proud of myself.

I stared at the old entertainment center that was centered between the windows of my front room. I couldn't watch my new TV without looking at the old one. For two weeks it sat there. I didn't want to pay that guy to come over again, and my neighbor was suddenly missing-in-action.

Every day when I looked at that entertainment center, I grew angrier. Angry at myself for not being able to do everything. Angry at my husband for not being around to get that thing out of my living room. Angry at the Army for sending him to the other side of the world. Angry enough to call the 111th Quartermaster Company. It was one of two Mortuary Affairs Units on constant rotation to Iraq and Afghanistan. Sergeant First Class Roman (who would later become acting first sergeant) answered the phone. He asked, "How may I help you, sir or ma'am?"

"My husband is in Balad," I said, "and if you really want to know how you can help me you can come get this darned entertainment center out of the middle of my living room."

"All right, ma'am. Who is your husband and where do you live? I'll need some directions to your house."

Guess who was at my door half an hour later on his lunch break? After SFC Roman moved my entertainment center and old television, he asked me how long it had been there. I guess he noticed the dust! When I told him it had been there for two weeks, he was genuinely upset. He chastised me for not having called sooner and told me to call his cell phone directly if there was anything I ever needed.

He talked with me on my front porch for almost an hour. He never said exactly how many separations his wife had endured during his military career, but I knew from the conversation that their marriage had survived many. He had an understanding of my feelings as a spouse that I never expected from a soldier. He spoke to me about trust, specifically the trust that my husband would be protected not only by the Army and his buddies, but by God. He asked me how I was handling the deployment, if I was having any trouble handling our finances, and whether I had anyone nearby that I could depend on during an emergency. He talked about the importance of having a plan in writing about who would care for my daughter should something happen to me during my husband's deployment. He offered phone numbers for his wife and other wives whose husbands were deployed. He gave me his cell phone number and those of other NCOs in my husband's unit in case I needed anything.

As he walked away, I felt like I had just spoken with an angel. He knew not just the logistics of having a husband deployed for the first time, but the feelings that came along with it. He talked to me about fidelity, commitment, and personal courage. He talked about the importance of my husband's job. I used this opportunity to ask him questions I had about the things I should say to my husband. Did I hold back my tears on the hard days so he wouldn't be worried about me, or did I let him know exactly how much I missed him and wanted him home? For the first time since my husband enlisted, SFC Roman made me feel like I was part of the Army family. Someone I had never even met (and his rank meant nothing to me) cared about my husband, my daughter, and me. He backed out of the driveway, and when I closed the door behind me, I felt less alone. I had reinforcements. In an unfamiliar post and city, I felt a sense of belonging and calm, the kind of calm you only feel when you are home.

DEVIN PATTON lives in Virginia with her husband (and hero) Bobby, daughter Madison, and their Pug, Suki. She is now the Family Readiness Group Leader for her husband's unit and enjoys target shooting, fundraising, and being room mom for her daughter's class.

The Family Forge
TERRI BARNES

In a blacksmith shop he built himself, on land that once belonged to his parents, and on an anvil inherited from his grandfather, my uncle forges a chain. He takes a rod, pliable and glowing from the forge, and bends it into a loop. He sprinkles Borax on the hot metal and explains that it will create a weld where the ends of the rod join to become the link of a chain.

"Better move back," he warns my children and me, before sealing the weld with his hammer. Pounding the Borax creates a shower of molten sparks. We "ooh" and "ah" like spectators at a fireworks display. I snap pictures like the tourist that I am, even among my own kin.

He repeats the process, forging the links together, three in all, imprinting them with his own mark, a small anvil-shape and his initials, and gives them to us. My aunt brings out a tray of iced tea, and we sit outside under the trees enjoying the shade on a hot July day.

We have just returned from an overseas tour, the second in our career as a military family. Two of our three children can scarcely remember visiting this place, but the memories are strong for me. The town where I grew up is less than a hundred miles away, and I spent many Saturdays and Sundays visiting my grandparents on this acreage, sharing meals full of vegetables from my grandparents' garden, climbing the hay bales in the barn, watching the hummingbirds in the mimosa tree in the backyard. All these I remember, but today's visit comes to an end too soon.

On another family visit, we take my grandmother out to lunch. There is a café in a small town near her house, the town where my parents and their brothers and sisters attended school and where some of their friends and families still live. The bell over the door announces our arrival. A girl and a boy run toward us. "Meemaw!" they cry, throwing their arms around my grandmother. Though I haven't seen them since they were babies, their faces—full of family resemblance—are immediately familiar to me. When I say hello, they smile shyly and cling to Meemaw's legs. "This is your Aunt Terri," she says, patting them on the back.

Their mother, my cousin's wife, is behind the counter. She says "Hi, Meemaw!" and to us, "We haven't seen y'all in a while." She is busy with a customer, but the kids sit down and have lunch with us, taking up with our three children like old friends. I wonder how old they will be before we see them again.

On the drive home, I remember my young cousins' effusive greetings to my grandmother and wish my children had that familiarity. But such relationships come only with constant tending and visits much more frequent than once a year or so.

In our mobile life, even visits to our families are nomadic. During vacation time or between assignments, we travel from place to place visiting our parents and siblings, forging the links of our extended family across eight states in two week's time. There is never enough time to see everyone—not enough to create the closeness I see between my more stationary relatives. But it is enough to remind us we are part of something larger than our family of five. Those links of family history are stretched by the geography of our military life, but they are strong. Those ties, those visits, however short, enrich our lives. They remind us that when we are on the other side of the world, there are people who love us and pray for us. They remind us that we are not alone. There are people out there who have my grandfather's nose and my mother's eyes and a familiar last name. There are people who remember the day I was born and the day I got married, the day I embarked on this journey.

The chain my uncle made is a reminder to us that those links are there, even when we are far away from the family forge.

TERRI BARNES is a lifelong military family member, first as a daughter, now as a spouse, and the mother of three grown-up military kids. A journalist and book editor, Terri is the author of *Spouse Calls: Messages from a Military Life* (Elva Resa, 2014), a best-of compilation from her long-running column in *Stars and Stripes*.

Vietnam and
Earlier Vintages

Flexible From the Beginning

CAROLE FRANCE

In 1961, I graduated from the University of Denver and was anticipating my upcoming marriage to John, a dashing fighter pilot. We'd been going steady for two years and, although he says he doesn't remember actually proposing to me, we were making plans for a September service.

I had ordered the wedding invitations. The ceremony would take place at Evans Chapel, a charming historic building on campus, and I booked the Tiffin Inn for a modest reception with punch, champagne, and finger foods. A friend of mine from work had offered to loan me her wedding dress, and I had coordinated with my two sisters to be bridesmaids. Everything was set.

Then the phone rang.

"Carole, it's John. I can't make it to our wedding after all." He had a joking tone but I didn't laugh. "We just got orders to gunnery school. I'll be gone."

I was stunned. We knew his Colorado Air National Guard unit had been activated by President Kennedy because of the Berlin Crisis. It was one of the reasons we decided to get married then. He'd have a job with a steady income for a year and we'd figure out what to do after that. I knew they'd have lots of work to get combat ready in their new aircraft. But I hadn't counted on this!

"It's our wedding, John" I said tearfully. "I've already made the plans."

"Just change 'em," he said. "What's the big deal?" It was his typical, all-business response. "The best man and the groomsmen have to go to gunnery school too, so that pretty much wipes out my side of the wedding party."

With that, he signed off and left me to wallow in misery. I immediately called my mother to unload.

"Listen, Carole," she said, ever the picture of stoic sensibility, "I know when you're 22-years old and this happens, you think it's the end of the world, but it's not. If it's the worst difficulty you have in life, you're a lucky woman."

Sniffle. "Our wedding," I whimpered.

"Get on the phone and reschedule everything."

I reluctantly began making calls. The only thing was, by then it was after 5 p.m. on Friday and nothing was open, not even the printer, and I couldn't stop the invitation order. I had to stew all weekend over matters before Monday morning when I could take up my grim work once again.

Two years earlier John caught my eye when he walked into my Philosophy class at the University of Denver. He was tall and handsome and older than the other male students. As the semester went by, some of us got into the habit of going to the YMCA after class. It was just a basement classroom furnished with secondhand sofas, but they sold coffee for five cents a cup.

Over coffee, I learned that John had been in the Air Force for five years. He'd flown the F-86 in Japan for two years and even did a stint as the left wing man in The Minutemen, the Air National Guard flight demonstration team which, in the fifties, rivaled the Thunderbirds and the Blue Angels.

"This guy is too worldly and sophisticated for me," I thought, trying to hide my crush. Then one rainy day as I trudged through the puddles on campus, John pulled up in his car and offered me a ride. He dropped me off at my next class and then out of the blue asked, "Would it be okay if I called you sometime?"

I waited constantly by the phone, willing it to ring. Finally on a Sunday morning it did.

"Would you like to go to Central City?" he asked, meaning a tourist/mining town in the mountains. Of course I did! That was the beginning of a two-year courtship during which we were practically inseparable.

I graduated from college and returned to my hometown of Great Falls, Montana, for a visit. John still had to finish his undergraduate work and, in the meantime, kept flying for the Colorado Air National Guard. The highlight of my summer was when he flew a training mission in an F-86 to Malmstrom

Air Force Base outside Great Falls and met my family. When he departed, he tipped his wings at us and my mother said it was the only time she'd gotten a personal fly-by. Rescheduling the wedding wasn't as hard as I thought. Both the chapel and the inn were available two weeks after our original date. The invitation order hadn't gone through, so I hastily made corrections. Everyone in the bridal party changed their calendars. Most importantly, my groom would be there.

Fresh from gunnery school, John was waiting for me as my younger brother escorted me down the aisle (my father was deceased). We exchanged vows in a simple ceremony. At the reception, the fighter pilots from John's squadron had such a good time that my mom had to pull the catering manager aside to order more champagne. "I can't believe how much these guys drink!" she said.

Fifty-four years later, John and I are still having a good time. It all started, we like to say, because of President Kennedy and the Berlin Crisis. But it lasted because I learned how to be flexible from the beginning.

CAROLE FRANCE and her husband spent over four decades with the Colorado Air National Guard. They were married 54 years until his death in 2015. Carole enjoys reading, sewing, and visiting her two daughters and three grandchildren.

Letters from Vietnam
JUDY HUNT RUDOLPH

September 15, 1961: *"I met Bill Rudolph. He has gorgeous sky blue eyes, long dark eyelashes, blonde hair, and a green '52 Ford. I liked him the minute I saw him. Wow!"*

That was a real diary entry written the night I met my future husband. I was 16 and he was 17; we lived in Mission, Texas, in the Lower Rio Grande Valley. Bill and I went steady during high school and got engaged in 1963 before college. He enlisted in the Army in February of 1966 and, because he was on orders for Vietnam, our plans for a big wedding were scrapped and we were married by a chaplain at Vance AFB in Enid, Oklahoma, on July 26, 1966. He had to report to California two weeks later for a flight to Vietnam.

The night before he left, I couldn't sleep. I wanted the clock to at least slow down, if not stop. All kinds of thoughts ran through my mind: what if this was the last night I ever slept with him? What if I never saw him alive again? What would I do if a green Army car pulled up in front of my parents' home? What would I do if he was KIA or a POW? How could he sleep so peacefully? Then again, maybe he wasn't sleeping so peacefully.

The next morning I tried to stay as cheerful as possible because I could tell he was anxious. He checked in at the flight line, came back out to make small talk, and before I knew it, he was kissing me goodbye through a chain link fence. As I watched my new husband walk up the ramp of a C-130, it seemed to swallow him. The plane ascended into the blue summer sky and I felt like my heart had been ripped out. There was actual physical pain. Exactly two weeks after our wedding, he was on his way to Vietnam. What a way to start a marriage!

Finishing my degree kept me busy while Bill was a door gunner on a Huey at An Khe with the 1st Cavalry Division. Back then, letters were the only communication we had and thankfully, he wrote every single day. I did not hear his voice for an entire year until he called from Alaska to say that he was on his way home. The call was short, but just hearing his voice was wonderful.

As we waited to welcome him at the airport, I was nervous and excited. My very wise mother said something that stayed with me all of our married life: "If you are ever mad at Bill about anything, always remember how excited and happy you are today." When he walked towards me, he looked so thin and gaunt, not the robust young man that I had sent off to Vietnam a year before. That first kiss and embrace were wonderful.

The first few days of being back together were awkward as we got to know each other again. It seemed as if I needed to back off and give him some space and time to adjust to being back in the real world. He slowly got used to being home after taking leave and assuming the responsibilities of a husband.

We were stationed at Fort Sill, Oklahoma, where I got my first teaching job at Geronimo Elementary School, but not before I had a job at the post laundry checking the pockets of old green fatigues. That was when soldiers field stripped cigarettes and put the debris in their pockets. Yuck! For this I went to four years of college?

When Bill first got home, I hand stitched his rank and new unit patches on his fatigues. I was so proud of myself, until he told me that I had sewn everything on upside down. What did I know? I was a young, naive Army wife. We could not afford to send his fatigues to the laundry, so every week I slaved over a hot iron and made sure that those creases were exact. My soldier was going to look sharp!

In October of 1969, he got sent to Vietnam again and I moved back to Enid, Oklahoma. I worked at a finance company to save enough money to meet him in Hawaii for one week of R&R in July of 1970. It was the most wonderful, romantic week. In four years of marriage, we had spent only one anniversary together, so that was very special.

I deeply regret what we did with all the letters Bill wrote during his two tours in Vietnam. Before he left, he destroyed all my letters. When he returned home, he burned every one of his. So many of our recorded thoughts and dreams went up in smoke. Those letters expressed his feelings while he was gone, as well as his observations on the world during those turbulent times. I was upset that he burned them, but I was so glad to have him home that I didn't protest.

When he came home from his second tour in 1970, he also burned the letters from that year. I should have stopped him, but I knew that he simply wanted to put the year behind us. I told him how sad I was that he burned our letters, but he has no regrets even today. It was a time in his life that he wants to forget.

It never occurred to me that those letters would tell our daughter about her parents and how they felt when they were young and separated by a war. Most of our letters were filled with what we did each day and what our dreams were. We discussed what we would do when he got home from Vietnam. I remember his letters were full of optimism; he really believed in the mission there. He spoke of the villagers and the small children he saw. He talked mostly about what a beautiful country it was and how he thought that we should be there doing something for the people.

Recently, my mother-in-law, Ann, found about 30 letters that Bill had written to her, and she asked if I wanted them. I was thrilled! Our daughter Barbie read them first. In an undated letter from his first tour, he wrote, *"Judy graduates on May 24. It is hard to believe she is finally graduating from college. I am really proud of her. I only wish I could be there to see it."* He said he was sending me pearls for college graduation. Our daughter realized those were the same pearls she wore to her wedding almost 30 years later.

Barbie said that the young man in the letters was so different from the man she knew as Dad. He is known as the pessimist of the family and the letters showed such optimism.

21 June 1966: Fort Eustis, Virginia: *"I am an E-2 now. It is an increase of $10 to $15 over E-1. If I stay straight I should become PF, which is a stripe pretty soon."*

On his 23rd birthday, 28 December 1966, he wrote: *"We*

had a *very good Christmas dinner and afterwards, the company had a softball game that lasted all afternoon long. The next day Bob Hope was here so the whole company got off work to see him. They'll be broadcasting the show on the 18th of January so don't forget to watch it. I wasn't sitting too far from the front."*

Friday, 26 August 1966: *"I am already counting the days until I go home."*

The dreams he talked about and the plans he had for the future were fun for Barbie to read. It's a window to a time that she has only read about in books or seen in movies. Finally, she knows about her Dad's connection to those events.

4 June 1970: *"Well, I only have six months left over here now. I feel like I am finally getting a little bit short. I now have a total of 18 months in Vietnam. I really believe that our push into Cambodia has shortened the war quite a bit, at least I hope that it has."*

In one of his early letters when he had only been in Vietnam for three weeks, he said, *"I'll have 18 months left in the Service when I finish my tour over here. I sure don't plan on re-enlisting in this Army. I want to go back to college and finish under the GI Bill."* This letter amused us because he came home one day at Fort Sill after his first tour and calmly announced that he had re-enlisted. We had never talked about making the Army a career, but that decision affected the next 22 years of our lives.

I am delighted that our daughter Barbie and grandchildren Cayden and Deklan have these letters that were written over 40 years ago. They give us insight into what kind of young man Bill was, the young man I fell in love with in 1961. He proudly served our country when he was needed and at a time when it wasn't popular to do so. How lucky we are that his mom found the letters and shared them with us. They are precious sheets of paper from a young man to his family in a time of war.

A native of Mission, Texas, JUDY HUNT RUDOLPH taught elementary school for 30 years in five states. After 24 years of Army life, her husband retired and they moved back to Texas in 1989. Bill died in 2016 and was buried on their 50th wedding anniversary with full military honors at Dallas/Fort Worth National Cemetery.

Many Good Men
NANCY DENTON

In December 1969 my husband Larry (now ex-husband), an Air Force helicopter pilot, was shot down in Cambodia and suffered a life-threatening head injury. He was flown to a field hospital in Vietnam where he had an emergency craniotomy. Once the doctors stabilized him, he was taken to a military hospital in Tachikawa, Japan. I left for Japan two days later.

Before Larry's tour to Vietnam, we decided that I would move with our two daughters (ages one and three) to my hometown of Overland Park, Kansas, a suburb of Kansas City. That decision was made because my family, Larry's parents and brother, and many childhood and college friends from the University of Kansas lived there, so my support system was in place. It was the right decision because when my husband was seriously injured, everyone rallied and looked after the girls so I could take care of Larry.

A Red Cross worker met me at the airport in Tokyo and we took a taxi to the hospital in Tachikawa (the driver only got lost once). The first time I saw Larry, he looked the same except there was a huge indentation on the left side of his forehead where a section of his skull had been removed. I could see his pulse throbbing in the indentation. He didn't recognize me and I don't think he ever knew who I was during the entire hospital stay in Japan. That didn't bother me so much. My thoughts were, "Thank God you don't know what's going on."

At that point we didn't know what to expect regarding Larry's condition. I listened to what the doctors told me and paid attention. Even though I was numb and in shock, I was remarkably calm. Larry looked okay, which was somewhat reassuring; he was moving and talking. Compared to some servicemen I saw with horrific burns or no arms or legs, I considered Larry one of the lucky ones. We were facing the unknown but I thought, "Let's see what happens."

I spent Christmas alone in a hotel that year. I remember watching television a week later and seeing the ball drop on Times Square. It was depressing but I could take it, all things considered. My daughters had Christmas in Kansas with family. During my absence, everyone took a week and stayed with them at my house so the children weren't uprooted.

After three weeks and two surgeries in Japan, including one to remove a blood clot, Larry was stable enough to move to the states. They loaded him on a C-141 full of gurneys—there must have been over one hundred patients along with flight surgeons and nurses—and air evacuated him to Wilford Hall in San Antonio, Texas.

At the Air Force Base in Texas, another Red Cross worker arrived to escort me to the hospital where I consulted with the Chief of Neurosurgery about Larry's prognosis.

"I'll be honest with you," he said. "The best you can hope for is he'll be a vegetable in a VA hospital. If he lives, that is." I was shocked by his lack of compassion. Larry's brother, a cardiologist, reamed the neurosurgeon for his poor bedside manner and the doctor later apologized to me.

Wilford Hall was a beautiful, big hospital. It was a fantastic community. The overworked nurses were excellent, and I felt the utmost respect for the military physicians. They were dedicated and top-of-the-line. (That aforementioned neurosurgeon was an SOB, but his abilities were unquestioned.)

I was at the hospital every day taking Larry to his physical therapy appointments and other treatments. We fought like hell to get him well. The nurses were glad to have family members there. The patients didn't have many visitors and they were starved for company, so I hung out with them in the lounges, played cards, watched TV, and listened to popular music. I had a support group; that's why I was there so much. I had enough money. Most of the patients were enlisted men and their families didn't have the resources to stay, so they were very lonely. It was sad.

One person who did visit Wilford Hall was Senator Bob Dole, a fellow Kansan and friend of my husband's family. Senator Dole was a Veteran who suffered a serious injury during his service to our country, and he had honest-to-God loyalty to anyone in the military. He spent some time at Larry's bedside, though Larry was in bad shape after his third craniotomy. I then accompanied the senator as he visited each ward. His kindness and concern for every patient remains with me to this day. When I introduced the senator, they were surprised to see him but they all knew who he was. There was nothing but enthusiasm for him. They gratefully shook his left hand because his right hand had been completely disabled during his own combat experience. The anti-war sentiment and demonstrations these young men had seen and heard after returning to the country they had so bravely defended suddenly disappeared.

"Thank you, Senator," they said. "It's an honor to serve." They were talking to one of their own. I can still see their faces and I will always remember the impact Senator Dole had on their lives. Their heartfelt thanks touched him to the core.

One young man was in a wheelchair with severe burns. His face was frozen with scar tissue and he couldn't even move his mouth to speak. Senator Dole knelt down next to his wheelchair and talked to him without expecting any response. Before long, tears started rolling down this young man's badly burned face. I was so moved I had to leave the room to compose myself. Senator Dole didn't have to do that, but his short visit made a huge impression on the patients.

I was in San Antonio for months after that. I stayed with Larry full-time for a while, and then flew home to spend time with the kids. Sometimes I brought the girls to see him on the weekends. The better he got, the less time I needed to stay at the hospital. His progress was off the charts. The staff was amazed. I learned later that the same doctor who had pronounced Larry "a vegetable" published a medical paper about his remarkable recovery.

Larry was released from Wilford Hall for good in late summer. He still took medication for seizures but those stopped eventually and he was able to drive again. We moved to Tempe, Arizona, where he got his Master's degree and a job with a pharmaceutical company. With excellent care and by sheer luck—and by being young and in good shape—Larry came back to us.

I haven't seen my ex-husband in years, but the memory of that moment upon arrival at the hospital in Japan will never fade. Thanks to so many dedicated doctors and military medical personnel, the word "hopeless" soon became "hopeful." In the end, another word summed it all up: "miraculous."

NANCY DENTON passed away of a heart condition in 2010. She is missed by her husband of 35 years, three daughters, seven grandchildren, and extended relatives and friends who remember her joie de vivre and devotion to family.

The Road Taken
BONNIE LEONARD

My brief stint as a military wife began in Athens, Georgia. Well, I suppose it actually started when I pinned on my fiancé's Ensign bars in a ceremony at Harvard College, where Jim was in Navy ROTC on a Holloway Scholarship. We were wed shortly thereafter, within two weeks of both his and my graduation.

I was following an unspoken, but clearly understood, life plan for girls at Wellesley College in the late 50s: engagement by Halloween of senior year followed by marriage soon after Commencement. A few far-sighted classmates went onto law school and even medical school, but they were rare. So when the faculty in the Geology department encouraged my application to graduate school, I declined politely with the quiet knowledge I was headed for marriage and motherhood.

But don't get me started on how inaccurately the movie *Mona Lisa Smile* portrayed the Wellesley of that generation. First of all, none of the faculty resembled Julia Roberts, although I must admit my Geology advisor's rugged good looks encouraged many an undergraduate to attend his classes. More importantly though, every professor challenged us to think for ourselves and it is silly to suggest that deportment classes on manners and grooming were part of the curriculum.

My Wellesley years became a memory when Jim and I were married on a warm day in June. We drove south in our second-hand green Ford with its unnecessary snow tires, headed for Athens, Georgia, where he would be attending Navy Supply Corps School. All our worldly belongings were packed in that car: in essence, our clothes and my grandmother's mah jongg set.

Truth be told, we headed north; it was not until we reached the Kittery Bridge, leading from New Hampshire into Maine, that Jim realized we were driving in the wrong direction. I, in complete oblivion, noticed nothing. Hindsight suggests we might have been coping in our own unique ways with some major life upheavals like finishing college, leaving home, moving to a new place, living together for the first time, and learning the unfamiliar roles of husband and wife. But in those days, the phrase "life transition" was not a part of the vernacular.

Georgia was a big change for this New England girl. It was hot, humid, and filled with red dirt. My knowledge that this soil derived from the Appalachian Mountains to the west brought little relief as we hunted for a place to live. Luckily, before long we found a high-ceilinged, furnished apartment on Prince Avenue directly across from the base.

And just like that, our married life began, in an unfamiliar town, far away from home, where everybody was a stranger. But this situation would change rapidly. In the summer of '59, hundreds of guys, fresh out of Navy ROTC programs from universities across the country, rolled into Athens to attend the Navy Supply Corps School, many of them with new wives.

Each weekday morning, the husbands headed off to school in 102-degree heat, while the wives headed for the pool. Sounds a bit unfair in retrospect, but we wives spent our evenings collating thousands of pages for logistical manuals and giving our husbands' shoes a military spit shine. We followed the local instructional lore, which was to polish with Kiwi black, buff well, and then swipe lightly with a five-day deodorant pad.

We were also cleaning house and learning how to cook. Neither was my forte, but I hastily mastered a shrimp fried rice recipe, which was exotic enough in those days to persuade dinner guests to return. If that did not do it, learning how to play mah jongg with my grandmother's tiles usually insured that bachelors and couples often found their way to our conveniently located apartment.

Molly and Wally were our most frequent guests. They both hailed from Stanford University and Molly and I quickly became fast friends. She already knew how to cook and could sew too. For my 22nd birthday in November, she surprised me with a handmade wool skirt. The warmth of that skirt was especially welcome on the cool Georgia piedmont in late fall.

But even more welcome was this heartfelt gift from a new friend.

After a few weeks by the pool that summer, I became so bored I began to wonder if the University of Georgia might need a Geology lab instructor for fall semester. Before my senior year in college, my department head and advisor had called me in to say, "You've been asking us questions for three years; now we think it's time someone asked you questions." My response to this surprising offer of a paid position as Lab Instructor for Geology 101 had been an unhesitating "Yes."

Things worked out just as easily when I called the head of the Geology Department at the University of Georgia. A doctoral candidate had left unexpectedly, so they were looking for someone to teach a freshman lab. I was hired on the spot in my interview with a warning not to be afraid "to flunk those East Georgia farm boys." Excitement ousted my boredom when I began teaching that group of go-get-'em southern girls and lackadaisical East Georgia farm boys.

In January, our time in Georgia came to a close. We then headed north to Boston where Jim was stationed on the *U.S.S. Macon*. Molly and Wally and their new infant were traveling with us as far as Washington, D.C. Molly had babies as effortlessly as she cooked and sewed. When her water broke, she called me to drive her to the hospital because Wally was in class. While she appeared incredibly relaxed, something told me to make tracks, so I cruised through a red light en route. Good thing too, because her daughter appeared within minutes of our arrival.

It was snowing at daybreak when our two families pulled out of Athens in that trusty, green Ford sedan loaded down with the goods of both households. Tucked snugly in the back were Molly, with her baby in a car bed beside her, and I, with a baby-to-be growing in my belly. In front, Jim was driving with Wally installed beside him as navigator.

Within an hour, it became obvious we were in the midst of a serious blizzard. Unlike any other car on the road, however, we had the benefit of those formerly unappreciated snow tires and an experienced cold weather driver. Jim had grown up on an island off the coast of Maine, where for winter entertainment he and his teenage buddies drove their fathers' cars down a hill and braked hard when they hit the frozen pond below. Handling skids was child's play for him.

So Jim and I bid farewell to our first Navy post, in a blizzard, only months after arriving in a heat wave. It was a meteorological metaphor for the radical life shifts we experienced during that short time. By adding motherhood to marriage, I had moved successfully forward on my consciously chosen life path. Unbeknownst to me, however, I had also taken a step towards a future career in higher education. But that ambition still lay buried in my unconscious and would not come knocking for another decade.

Serving as Dean of Continuing Education at Wellesley College for 20 years, and in her current capacity as a Certified Life Coach, BONNIE LEONARD has devoted her career to empowering women. She has guided hundreds of clients through life's transitions, helping them to create more purposeful, rewarding, and exciting lives. Her book, *Midlife Magic: The Seven Day Self-Care Plan to Boost Your Energy and Make You Smile* was recently published by Stillwater River Press. Find out more at www.bonnieleonard.com.

A Great Trip Together
LOUISE SMITH

On August 17, 1939 at 5:45 p.m., Stan and I were married at my parents' summer cottage in New Castle, New Hampshire. The time had something to do with the tide, as after our reception at Portsmouth Yacht Club, we crossed the Piscataqua River by boat to Kittery, Maine, where we'd left our packed car that morning. Thus began my life as an Army wife. My new husband Stan had graduated from the U.S. Military Academy in 1937 as First Captain of The Corps.

After a short honeymoon in Quebec, we arrived at the Thayer Hotel in West Point where Stan had a temporary duty to coach football. We were assigned two adjoining hotel rooms. Two events stand out in my memory. First, washing Stan's handkerchiefs and plastering them to the mirrors so ironing would not be necessary and second, keeping a diaphragm on the window sill. Neither was successful!

The end of football season found Stan reporting to Governors Island, New York, as a company officer with the 16th Infantry. We were assigned quarters in the old jail house where the kitchen, dining room, and living room were in the basement. Two bedrooms and a bath were on the first floor. The first incident I remember here was a doctor telling me I was pregnant. Secondly, we had been royally entertained by other Army folks, so we decided to host a cocktail party with another Army couple we had met. We bought a case of gin. At the end of the party we discovered 25 of us had consumed a total of half a bottle of gin. That must have been quite a party!

Shortly after that "majestic" success, Stan decided he was better suited for a teaching career, so he resigned from the Army and spent a year at university taking more Education courses. He then entered the Coast Guard and reported to the Coast Guard Academy in New London, Connecticut, to teach Math and coach football.

Then came World War II and duty called. A trip to Washington transferred Stan back to the Army. The young officer who handled this transfer was none other than Major Dwight D. Eisenhower! By this time we had a wonderful son, Stanley Smith Jr., whom we called "The General."

Stan's first assignment was to the Fort Knox Armor School and then to the 20th Armored Division as a light tank company commander, later promoted to S-3, 20th Armored Regiment. This involved a move to Clarksville, Tennessee, and our first home.

Our first rental there was in the center of town in an old southern, one-story home occupied by huge rats. Upon our arrival, a helpful neighbor told us to watch the baby carefully as rats might attack if they smelled milk on him. Needless to say, I slept little in this house! Stan left early each day for the training fields. One morning I rose to get the baby's milk from the refrigerator, but between me and the refrigerator sat a huge rat staring me down. The baby and I quickly snuggled back in my bed and cried together for a couple of hours. When we approached the kitchen again the rat was still there. Deciding he was dead, I gave the rodent a huge kick and marched to the refrigerator to find a bottle for my hungry baby. That night as I sobbed my story to Stan, he laughingly said he too had seen the rat and left the house by a different door, assuming the rat would depart by the time I woke up. I announced that if he didn't make arrangements to leave the rat house, the baby and I would return to Connecticut. He made the arrangements.

An enterprising real estate mogul had thrown together some small salt box homes which he was selling for a $200 down payment. Still lacking funds, we called on my maternal grandmother, our greatest source of revenue through the years, who loaned us the money. (When we left Tenessee for Georgia we "sold" our home for $200 and I don't remember paying my grandmother back.) We hired a man and his horse and plow to dig up a huge garden. Although we got it planted (our first of many wonderful gardens), the Tennessee sun and heat made it impossible for us to work in it, so the garden died a dismal death.

My mother knew someone who knew someone who knew someone who lived in Clarksville, Tennessee. Eventually news reached "Mrs. Someone" that Louise Smith, young Army wife, had arrived in Clarksville and should be entertained. A formal invitation arrived in my mail for a luncheon. I foolishly accepted. I arrived in a much too informal outfit, but worst of all, with bare, suntanned hands and all the other guests wore white gloves. I tried keeping my hands out of sight by hiding them behind my back or sitting on them. Nothing worked. The guests wore their gloves to the luncheon table. Not until the maid had the first course in place did they ceremonially remove their gloves and begin to eat.

Afterwards, I bought some special stationery to write my thank you note. But I also decided not to return the luncheon invitation in our home where orange crates served as living room tables and mismatched rented furniture was found in the rest of the house. (The two dollar a month brass bed was marvelous!)

Not long after the luncheon, Stan was assigned to Fort Benning, Georgia, where we rented a small, two-bedroom house in Columbus, already inhabited with an extraordinary number of cockroaches. Plagued with a lack of money as usual, we rented our second bedroom to a young soldier and his wife, who shared a bathroom with us and the roaches. All went well until Stan discovered the young soldier's wife was using *his* razor to shave her legs, resulting in language I best not record here!

Soon after that, orders came through for Stan to return to West Point to become a company tactics officer and instructor in armored tactics in warfare. Our housing problems ended with very lovely quarters at West Point. We were assigned a big house with four bedrooms and a couple of bathrooms. A daughter, Susan, was born in June 1944. Since no one had heard of health benefits back then, we were very fortunate that she was born at West Point where we were charged only a dollar a day for an 11-day stay. While hospitalized I took my very first shower. Saturday night tub baths were in style back then.

Following WWII, Stan returned to the U.S. Coast Guard Academy where he ended his career there as Dean of the Academy. Following that retirement he became Director (President) of the Avery Point branch of the University of Connecticut. Being the dear husband that he was, he retired in 1975 to care for me after colon cancer left me with a prognosis of six months to live. We are still waiting. So, my friends, *never* give up. Since then we have had a beautiful life of travel and love at our home in Mystic, Connecticut.

In August 2006 we happily moved to a senior retirement home in Groton, Connecticut. Many relatives will help me celebrate my 90th birthday and our 68th wedding anniversary in 2007. It's been a great trip together. Thank you, God, Army, and the Coast Guard.

Although saddened by Stan's death in late 2007, LOUISE SMITH celebrated his 93 years of life with their 5 children, 10 grandchildren and 13 great-grandchildren. Determined to be an "interesting widow," she started taking organ lessons and made plans to attend her 70th reunion at Wellesley College. Louise passed away in 2008.

Considering Loss

The Little Manila Envelope
ANDI HURLEY

The night before my husband deployed, he nonchalantly handed me a little manila envelope. On that night, we didn't acknowledge its contents, but I was fully aware of what was stuffed inside. There was an updated will, a living will, insurance paperwork, a Power of Attorney and, though I never checked, I'm sure it also included a letter to me, "just in case."

I didn't hide the envelope; I left it out so that it could easily be grabbed by me, or anyone else "just in case." The envelope was in a basket by my desk, so each time I sat down to work on the computer, I was reminded of the scenario that all spouses fear. But still, the envelope needed to be within easy grasp, so it stayed there, "just in case."

A few weeks after my husband left, I remembered the story of a friend of mine, a soldier's mother who had to abruptly fly to Germany after her son was injured by a Vehicle-borne Improvised Explosive Device (VBIED) in Iraq. Some time after he was injured, she gave public advice on preparedness. *Keep your passport handy,* she said. My passport was in a different location from the little manila envelope. So late one night, I retrieved my passport from its usual file and I slipped it into the envelope with the other papers. That marked the first time I had touched the little manila envelope since my husband handed it to me.

There would be one more occasion which forced me to handle the little manila envelope while my husband was away. I needed the new Power of Attorney for a real estate transaction. I hated to touch the envelope, but I reached inside and found what I needed pretty quickly, but not before seeing another document which was official-looking, clearly labeled and folded a perfect tri-fold. A *Last Will and Testament.* I didn't dig any further after putting my hands on the document I needed. I didn't want to.

We are all aware of the dangers our spouses face, and we

have to be practical, organized, ready and prepared for the worst-case scenario. I'm sure each of us has different things which remind us of the danger and which trigger emotions that aren't always easy to deal with. Mine was that little manila envelope. Although I had a clear understanding of everything that was stated on the pages of those legal documents, I didn't like the envelope that contained all of the directives. Actually, I hated it. It was *toxic*. It had "beware" and "danger" written all over it. It could have been a file, or a box or anything else, and my revulsion would be the same. But, as it happened, it was a little manila envelope.

Funny, when my husband came home, I never gave that envelope a second thought. It sat in the basket for weeks, all but invisible to me. The little manila envelope could no longer affect me. Thankfully, I never needed it.

A few weeks ago, I nonchalantly handed the envelope back to my husband. It felt good. We didn't acknowledge its contents. No words were exchanged. I've never asked my husband what he did with the envelope. I'm sure it will come back to me at some point. For now, I'm rather enjoying not having it within reach.

ANDI HURLEY'S husband recently retired from the U.S. Army, and they were thrilled to plant permanent roots in Florida. During their time as an Army family, they moved 15 times in 24 years. Andi now applies her experiences and creativity as a professional home stager to help owners prepare their properties for market.

Sorority Sisters
SUSAN HOOD FRANZ

A lady I'd never met walked up to me and said, "I hear we are members of the same sorority." I looked at her quizzically, wondering how she in her early 60s, and I in my late 30s, could have been in the same sorority. I said, "Really? Phi Mu?" With tears in her eyes, she shook her head and said, "No dear, the sorority you never asked to be in and the one you can't get out of." She explained further, "My husband died and left me with three small children when I was very young."

I was 37 years old, seven months into widowhood, and the mom of a strong-willed two-and-a-half-year-old boy when I met this sorority sister. I was just beginning to rebuild a life that had suddenly changed forever. My husband, a major in the Army, had died of a brief, unexpected illness six weeks after we moved to Fayetteville, North Carolina. We had just bought our first home and had already begun to make changes to it. He had started his dream job, we had a beautiful child, and we were only four hours away from my parents. All seemed perfect.

Instead of the life I had envisioned, I returned to the church garden to bury his ashes in the same place where we had posed for our wedding pictures 12 years earlier. Seven months later, after selling my house and settling affairs, my son and I moved in with my parents until I could make a new plan for our lives. In this new place I found out the meaning of being a "sorority sister."

Looking back on the experience is something I try not to do very often. I like to live in the present and look to the future, but some things truly stand out in my mind about that time. To this day I would say it felt as if someone had dropped a bomb in my life, blowing it to pieces. I was surprised at how much my identity was associated with my husband. I was suddenly nobody. At least I felt that way when, about two weeks after my husband's death, I had to get a new military ID card. This time it annotated my husband as "deceased" rather than "active duty." I cried so hard that day right in the ID card office. I'm not sure why I had to change my card because nobody ever noticed the "DEC" on the card, indicating his status. Usually after showing my card, I was asked "What unit is your husband in?" or "What's his phone number?" I hated having to say "He's dead." "Oh ...," they would say in embarrassment and regret.

Dinner time was the worst time of day for me. I had always enjoyed watching my handsome husband drive up in his truck after work. I looked forward to his kiss and a recap of his day. Now I was left with no one to talk to and dinner preparations for a toddler and me. It was very depressing. One evening, I called a friend to see if she could watch my son the next day. Soon into our conversation she started whining about her husband working late hours and never being home to help. I couldn't believe she was so insensitive. In my disbelief I said nothing. Today I would remind her that at least she had a husband to be angry at and to cook for. I didn't say anything then and we no longer have a relationship now anyway.

One bittersweet memory I have is when, a few days after his death, two couples who were friends of ours came to help pack my husband's clothes. I asked for their help because I just couldn't look at his uniforms in the closet and believe he was dead. They brought some wine, and the girls and I sat on my couch and drank and reminisced with much laughing and crying. The guys, Desert Storm buddies, got the packing done and found a few keepsakes. What a blessing to have that time together to celebrate his life and to help me move on.

I find it difficult now to hear about Army friends being promoted or getting a command, although I'm happy for them. Each time I hear the good news, I'm forced to think about where my husband might be if he had lived and what he missed. From a selfish standpoint, I've been spared the pain of multiple deployments possibly resulting in death or injury in Iraq or Afghanistan. Nevertheless, I loved the military as much as my husband did and I can't hear "I'm Proud to be an American" without dissolving into tears.

I'm a different person today because of my experience. I have a hard time connecting with anyone who hasn't experienced some sort of life tragedy. That carefree self that I was and the attitude I used to have is gone. I had always been used to life going *my* way. This was the first time that I had to face the reality that there were things in life I couldn't control no matter how organized, intelligent, or faithful I was. I'm thankful to have awakened from my selfish sleep. I value life so much more and can relate to others facing similar issues. Although I would never have chosen the experience, it has made me a better person because it has changed my perspective on life. My best friend since this experience is a woman whose son almost died at birth from a disease. Her son is now my son's best friend. My girlfriend and I connect on a different level that is inexplicable to others without similar experiences.

The sorority I belong to is increasing in size. Maybe you know one of my sisters. Many of them didn't have the chance to say goodbye as I did. If you encounter one of them, be sensitive. Even if your husband is a true ogre, don't complain about him to one of my sorority sisters. Ask her if you can watch her kids so she can run some errands. Invite her to dinner and try to steer the conversation to other things besides who is getting promoted and what you're wearing to the next military ball. Find out what is the worst time of day for her and do something to help get her through it. If you know other sorority sisters that you can introduce her to, do it. If you are one of my sisters, help a newly initiated sister. While I was still living in Fayetteville, I was providentially introduced to two other sisters. The bond of shared experience eclipsed friendship and made us what we are, sisters in a sorority we never asked to be in.

SUSAN HOOD FRANZ, a U.S. Army, Army National Guard, and Air Force Reserve veteran, lives in Williamsburg, Virginia, with her husband of thirteen years and their two college-aged sons. She spends her time volunteering for several organizations and flipping houses with her husband and father. For fun she loves to paddleboard, hike, bike, camp, and travel.

Will I See You Tomorrow?
PHYLLIS WARD

One day while I was browsing the *In Touch Ministries* website, a picture of a small child in a missionary program grabbed my attention. I wanted to go on a mission trip. I've always felt there was more I was supposed to be doing for God besides my day-to-day routine.

I began to assess my skills. Even though I read the bible daily, I didn't feel my memory of scripture was adequate for mission work. My background and passion were fitness and the military. What in the world would I do with that?

I googled a search for "jobs in Iraq" and pulled up a well-known contractor that works in Iraq. I searched their site for jobs and saw "MWR Coordinator." Interesting—I worked for Morale, Welfare, and Recreation at Fort Leonard Wood, Missouri.

I read the job description of an MWR Coordinator and it was exactly what I was already doing. I thought, "You mean they do this in Iraq?" You could have knocked me over with a feather.

I talked to my husband about going to Iraq to serve our troops for a year. You could have knocked *him* over with a feather but he said, "Go for it."

I've been married to the military for 12 years now and have gone through two deployments and numerous moves with my husband. We are coming up on his retirement after 23 years and, after being a compliant Army wife (most of the time), I deployed to Fallujah, Iraq.

I worked the 1000-2230 shift at the internet café in Fallujah. We had a crowd of Marines and soldiers sitting in the waiting area for their turn to use the phones and computers.

Each night I made popcorn and put on a movie. The troops followed the smell of the popcorn and meekly approached me asking, "Ma'am, that popcorn sure does smell good. May I have some?"

As I cleaned up and went in the waiting area, I looked over the room of about 30 troops while they laughed, ate popcorn, and enjoyed the movie. I felt like I had a room full of sons and daughters and my family was in from missions. They were safe and sound under my watchful eye.

I thought about their mothers and fathers. What were they doing right now? I knew they must worry each day about their children. Even though the service members were technically adults, they were someone's children.

I found myself wishing I had a camera so that I could film each one of them and send it to their parents or write each one a letter to let them know that their kids were safe and sound.

I'm always amazed how quickly our troops can switch gears. They are trained to do battle, but as they sat in the café, they laughed, played games, watched movies, and kept in contact with their families through email and by phone.

They were very appreciative of the support they received from people in the United States. They easily talked about their families and spoke lovingly of them. They knew this time in Iraq wasn't forever and they'd return home after their deployment.

At that moment they were peaceful, happy, and free from danger.

As I surveyed the room I once again thought of their parents. *Mothers and fathers*, I thought, *I'm watching over your children right now.*

I wanted to hug each one of them. I wanted to pray with each one of them to let them know that they don't have to go through this deployment alone, to tell them that God loves them and to pray God's protection upon them.

I thought of the real possibility that I would not see them again and began to wonder, "Will I see you tomorrow?" Some of these kids I knew well. Most of them I saw everyday. I had great admiration and respect for all of them.

I talked with one young Marine Corporal who had his dog Lex with him. I wanted to take a picture of the two of them together but CPL Dustin Lee wasn't sure how Lex would react since they had just experienced an explosion that day.

Lex was a big, beautiful German Shepherd, a bomb sniffing dog. He was large but not intimidating. Even while at rest, Lex was very attentive and constantly looked to his handler for direction.

I asked CPL Lee if I could pet his dog and he said yes. I missed my Pekingese mix dog at home so I grabbed every opportunity to make a new canine friend. The "war dog" Lex suddenly turned into a big marshmallow. He was no longer on duty. Lex's reward for military service was all the attention he could handle, and he lapped up every bit of it.

I spoke with CPL Lee a little while longer. A tall, handsome young man, he struck me as an "All-American Kid." He had "the Few, the Proud, the Marines" look about him. Always quick to smile and very friendly, he had participated in many of our Fun Runs with his friends. I couldn't help but think that his parents must be very proud of him.

CPL Lee told me that he and his dog were going back to the states soon and how excited he was. He was stationed at Camp LeJeune, North Carolina, but Mississippi was home. His dog Lex was a seven-year veteran and was retiring upon his return from Iraq.

He was obviously very proud of his dog, always reaching down to pet him as he talked. It was also obvious that Lex had great admiration for CPL Lee because he never took his eyes off him. In fact, Lex was going home with CPL Lee to become his pet.

Weeks later I heard my supervisor, also a dog lover, mention that Lex had taken shrapnel during an explosion. I asked about the dog and she said he was on his way back to the states; he was okay.

She seemed to leave out the most obvious information that I would want to know. If the dog was injured, what happened to the dog handler? I swallowed hard and asked the question.

"I thought you knew," she said. "CPL Lee was killed."

I was angry, hurt, shocked, but most of all I didn't want to believe it. One of my boys was dead. I'd never see him again.

He was only 20 years old! This made no sense at all! I left the gym to be by myself. I didn't want the troops to see me so upset. I cried and sobbed until I had nothing left in me.

I later found out that Lex and CPL Lee were standing by a concrete wall that was hit by a mortar. Lex was the last one to see his handler alive. Even though Lex was injured he lay with CPL Lee and licked his face as if trying to revive him. It was too late. All the love in the world could not bring CPL Lee back.

How must his parents feel? Their son was so close to coming home and now they would never see him again. I knew they must have felt so helpless because they couldn't be there and hold him in their arms once more. They would never see his beautiful smile again.

I also knew that they must have been very proud of him. CPL Dustin Lee walked his talk. Many of us talk about the unrighteousness in this world but he did something about it. He served his country. He was a Marine!

I don't think I will ever forget that night. The memory will live on in my heart forever. I am so proud of our young men and women and I will continue to pray over them with these words from Psalm 91, which my friend prays over me each day:

> I will say of the LORD, "He is my refuge and my fortress, my God, in whom I trust ..."

> He will cover you with his feathers,
> And under his wings you will find refuge;
> His faithfulness will be your shield and rampart.

Months after CPL Lee's death, I received an email from an organization telling me that Dustin's family was not allowed to adopt Lex, who was still working in Georgia training other military dogs. He wasn't deployable, but he was still working.

A petition was set forth to release Lex to the Lee family. The Lees worked relentlessly for the adoption of Lex.

This story does have a happy ending. Nine months later,

CPL Lee's aunt emailed the news that Lex was being released to the Lee family. They picked him up in Georgia on December 21, 2007. Lex was home for Christmas.

I read in an article that releasing a working dog to someone besides the dog handler is unheard of. In this season of miracles it reminds one that all things are possible with God.

I believe that CPL Lee must be looking down from his mansion in heaven and flashing one of his beautiful smiles. He is at peace and can rest assured that his beloved Lex has a wonderful new home with his family.

PHYLLIS WARD served the Marine Corps in Iraq by creating sports, fitness, and recreation programs for the troops. She has written an inspirational book called *God's Temple: 40 Days to Total Transformation* (available on Amazon.com), and has many published fitness articles online.

A Few Terrifying Moments
KRIS JOHNSON

In June 2003, my husband took command of an Infantry battalion in the 101st Airborne Division, the famed "Screaming Eagles." He joined the battalion already in Iraq while I made the move with our two children to Fort Campbell, Kentucky, without him. Timing was not on our side. I did the entire move from Fort Bragg, North Carolina, alone and unpacked every ounce of our 17,540 pounds of household goods myself.

We started the "battalion command team" process on separate playing fields. With the battalion already deployed, I inherited the family support systems that were in place. I was thrown into the fire, but I didn't want wives to think I was burning. The first coffee I held in July had an inauspicious beginning. The wives were anticipating their husbands' return by the end of summer, and I had to tell them not to expect it before Christmas. There were a lot of sad faces at that coffee.

As the battalion commander's wife, I volunteered to attend monthly post meetings and pass on the information to the Family Readiness Group leaders at the company level. I also fielded a lot of phone calls, coordinated meetings, and answered questions from wives and parents. I was busy all the time.

We did our best in those early days of the war, but found much to improve upon, particularly the casualty and death notifications procedures. One time a wife got a call from a sergeant at the military hospital in Landstuhl, Germany, announcing her husband was on life support. A flurry of phone calls followed and we confirmed that he was on a ventilator, which in medical-speak is "life support," but he wasn't as close to death as it sounded. The sergeant was only following his protocol, but the hospital and battalion had two different communication loops.

Our battalion had a few men wounded, but no casualties. One of the injured soldiers was a company commander who had been critically wounded in one of the first IED incidents involving the 101st. "IED" was a new acronym in the Fall of 2003 but we all quickly learned what it meant: "Improvised Explosive Device." Initially, the soldier's survival was questionable because of his extensive injuries. His wife was the first family member in our battalion to go to Landstuhl, Germany, to be with her husband using "Invitational Travel Orders," something the Army gives only in severe cases when the doctors feel the presence of family could make a life-or-death difference. Sure enough, when she got to her husband's bedside, he sensed her touch and presence and within 45 minutes his vital signs improved.

As I said, notifications were challenging in the beginning, but the Army quickly got a handle on them. After the family was officially notified of an injury, I followed up with a phone call a few hours later. I tried to guide them through the initial shock and help them understand what was going on. I answered questions, prepared them mentally, and reassured them. I got through it all with composure because I had to; I didn't want the families to fall apart. Sometimes later on I'd have a good cry in private, but I prided myself on being calm and cool in the moment.

One Sunday evening in the fall, I was puttering in the kitchen, getting organized for the week ahead, planning school lunches, and doing the other tasks that never ended. My mind was far from the war in Iraq. I had a home and family to care for, and the issues with our unit families and wounded soldiers were at a lull for the first time in a long while. My thoughts were interrupted by a knock on the door. I looked out my window and froze in my tracks. There was a white SUV parked in my driveway, a Military Police vehicle. The kitchen door was open and I saw a soldier in BDUs, standing alone, looking at me through the screen door. My heart pounded. Rational thought processes shut down and panic gripped me. Time shifted to super-slow motion.

I drifted toward the screen door in a haze. Unless it's an ever-present reality in your life, you have no idea what finding someone at your door in uniform can mean.

"Good evening, Ma'am," said the soldier. "I just stopped to tell you the interior lights in your car are on."

"What?" I asked dimly, still paralyzed with dread.

"The interior lights in your car are on," he repeated. "Better turn them off. Your car won't start tomorrow."

He was only here to save me from a drained car battery! My eyes filled with tears and I practically collapsed with relief as I let out the biggest sigh he or I had probably ever heard.

"Do you know what you just did to me?" I asked him sharply. I explained why I had such a dramatic reaction. With the recent casualties in my husband's battalion, I had immediately jumped to the conclusion that he was bringing me more bad news, bad news of a very personal nature. Even today, as I recall this incident of five years ago to commit it to paper, my palms sweat and my pulse races. The entire event lasted maybe two minutes, but it seared an impression on my heart. It reminded me of a scene in the movie *We Were Soldiers Once* when the colonel's wife answered her door to see the taxi driver asking for her by name with a casualty telegram in his hand.

I felt bad for this young soldier as I laid my heavy emotional stuff on him when he had only stopped on a Good Samaritan mission. He was sincerely apologetic, but I shouldn't have let my mind race irrationally. I *knew* how these notifications were done. I was the one who taught the younger Army wives about this stuff. But reason had escaped me for a moment.

Our battalion's policy for seriously wounded soldiers was to notify the family in person if at all possible instead of by phone. The Rear Detachment commander didn't wear his Class A uniform (the Army's green dress uniform) to notify the family of an injury. He wore his BDUs, his daily duty uniform. The Casualty Notification Officer dressed in Class A uniform to deliver the ultimate bad news of a death. And he certainly would go to the front door, not the kitchen door. This was a big distinction for how bad news was delivered. I knew all this, but didn't process it. Rational thought left me for a terrifying moment.

I'm hard on myself—it was only a human moment—but

it's a mistake I never made again. I couldn't allow myself to fall apart as a leader. This doesn't mean that I believe my husband is indestructible. A bearer of bad news can appear at my door any time while he is off doing "that Army thing." But I knew with 750 families looking to me, the experienced mother hen of the unit, I had to stay strong to give them confidence that competent and compassionate advice and guidance were just a phone call away. That's what I looked for in the battalion commander's wife when I was a young Army bride. Now it was my turn to set the example in the best way I could. So, if an Army wife at Fort Campbell ends up with a dead car battery because the military police were afraid to knock on her door, she can blame me!

KRIS JOHNSON was commissioned in the U.S. Army Reserves and is a graduate of the U.S. Army Airborne School. She attended multiple leadership courses and has received numerous awards, to include the Commander's Award for Civilian Service, the Commander's Award for Public Service, the Department of the Army Outstanding Civilian Service Medal, and the Molly Pitcher Award. After the courts martial of her ex-husband, she became an advocate for military spouses and families who are in jeopardy of losing access to military retirement pay and benefits because of service member misconduct. She is currently a Constituent Services Liaison for a Congressman in North Carolina. The mother of two grown children, Ms. Johnson lives in Fayetteville and likes to say that she "got the house, the friends, and the Army" in her divorce.

Home, Hearth, and Holidays

The Incredible Shrinking Quarters
SHEILA FARRELL

Kevin and I began our life as an Army couple in a roomy, five-bedroom, split-level house in Colorado Springs, Colorado. It was a rental just outside the gates of Fort Carson and it had the works—three bathrooms, two car garage, and built-in lawn sprinkler system. For newlyweds with no kids, we were "living large." Earlier we had driven on post to check out available quarters, but I took one look at the squat ugly duplexes and said, "No thanks." After seeing Army housing for 20 years, I now know those duplexes were pretty nice.

After Fort Carson, Kevin's next orders took him to graduate school at Columbia University in New York City. We searched and searched for an apartment in the city, but on his pay we couldn't afford to live near the campus without settling for a dump. Instead, my in-laws invited us to live on the third floor of their house, a modest Tudor-style home in Harrison, New York, about 40 minutes from Columbia. For two years we stayed in a space that was originally an attic but had been converted into two small rooms and a half bath under the eaves. We had to go downstairs to take a shower. It wasn't an ideal situation, and especially after our first child, Elizabeth, was born, marital tensions escalated.

Then Kevin was assigned to the U.S. Military Academy as an instructor in the History department. Our home was a 600-square foot, two-bedroom apartment within walking distance of his office. Granted, it was small (the kitchen was tiny) but it had a fireplace, crown moldings, and a magnificent view of the Hudson River. Dating back to the 1920s, the building also had the charming history of being former nurses' quarters for the old hospital.

Soon I became pregnant with our second child and we needed larger quarters. We had to move ourselves to another house on post, an unattractive 70s-era duplex with a big kitchen and four bedrooms. It was a split-level design so when

I was in the kitchen, I looked up to ground level. It was sort of like Laverne and Shirley's apartment; I could see people's feet walking by my window. It reminded me of a cave, but I was happy to have the space so both kids could have their own bedroom.

All the extra space went away with our next move to Fort Leavenworth, Kansas, for a ten-month school. Like the other students, we were packed into cramped, three-bedroom town homes. It's not an exaggeration to say we were camping out there, surrounded by bare bulbs, cinderblock walls, and peeling linoleum floors. The unfinished basement, where we stored much of our stuff, had warnings stenciled on the wall: "Caution: Basement Floods." Nice. With large brown dumpsters at regular intervals along the street and no grass in sight, we said the neighborhood looked like the "projects," except the cars were nicer.

Then we went to Schweinfurt, Germany, where we anticipated stairwell living. Luckily, we got assigned a house instead. It had four bedrooms, a basement playroom, and the living room/dining room combination that the Army loves. For two years in Germany we actually had a guest room for family and visitors who visited us overseas.

Our good luck continued when we were re-assigned to Fort Leavenworth, Kansas, where our third child was born. This time Kevin was an aide-de-camp and we had designated quarters right next to the General's 9000-square foot house. Ours was one third the size, but still the most beautiful housing we'd ever lived in. The wide front foyer led to a staircase with a banister and landing. There was also a second set of stairs off the butler's pantry. Both the living room and dining rooms had fireplaces and sliding pocket doors. Although we had only one full bathroom, we spread out in the four bedrooms and the basement office, where we kept a pull-out sofa. (The basement also turned out to be a good place to hide during tornado warnings.)

We got spoiled with all that room, but our luck didn't last. We went from a roomy house to a small one when we moved to Fort Stewart, Georgia. Kevin was to be a battalion com-

mander in charge of 900 soldiers, so we lived on post in designated quarters. I felt like crying when I first set eyes on that
1200-square foot ranch house with vinyl siding. It looked like
a double-wide trailer! I peeked in the windows and really had
to fight back tears. There was dark gray carpeting throughout,
badly stained in the dining room with a bleach trail going
down the hall. It was depressing. I was so disappointed. (They
later replaced the carpet.) Kevin finally got the command he'd
dreamed of for 20 years and we got this terrible house to go
with it. It had a narrow galley kitchen with the washer and
dryer at one end. I joked that I could fold clothes and stir the
pot of macaroni and cheese at the same time. The other houses
on the street had carports but ours didn't. We had to purchase
a steel-framed canvas shelter to protect our cars from the
Georgia pine tar. Frankly, it looked tacky but came in handy
when we had battalion get-togethers.

Before we moved from Kansas, we put as much stuff as
we could into storage, but we still had to call for a second
storage pick-up after our household goods were delivered to
Georgia. Since we didn't have a basement or attic for boxes,
we also rented a private storage locker for things like Christmas
decorations and military collectibles. One way or another we
fit our family of five into the little house. With Kevin deployed
to Iraq for a year, we had one less person in the house most of
the time.

Like me when I was a newlywed, many of the younger
wives lived off post in new developments. Just about everyone
in the battalion had larger and nicer homes than we did. When
they came to our house for social functions, some of them
later told me they were shocked. "It's so small. Is this what
you get after 20 years in the Army?" they asked. I had to admit
it was. What could we do but make the most of it? I focused
on the positive things, like nice neighbors, a playground
nearby, and a laundry room that wasn't in the basement.

It has been over 20 years since I began my life in the military as a wife. Adapting to different sizes and shapes of houses
is only one aspect of the challenges we face as we follow our
soldiers around the world. Through it all I've come to realize

that it's not the houses we live in, but the homes we make for our families that really matter.

SHEILA FARRELL has been married to Kevin since 1990, and they have three children. She enjoys oil painting and tennis in her free time. After years of living in government quarters, they bought their first house when Kevin retired in 2013.

Hooah Chic
ANGELA OWENS

Last year, much to my surprise, I was asked to feature my home on the Christmas Tour of Homes. For those who don't know, it's a holiday fundraiser that allows people to tour certain homes during the season.

I'm a realist. I knew that this had nothing to do with my decorating prowess. I have four children, three pets, and, I'm the first to admit, the artistic ability of a rock. I'm what you'd call decorating challenged. Because we lived in one of the more unique—OK, big—sets of quarters on Fort Polk, people were curious. I understood that they wanted to see my "house" more than the "home" I'd tried to create with my half-baked, HGTV projects.

Nevertheless, panic ensued. Obviously, I would have to clean. I mean PCS-style clean. Also, I would have to actually decorate for the holidays. We'd been stationed in Europe for the previous three years and had traveled each Christmas. Other than the perfunctory door wreath, I was seriously out of practice hanging garland. I was facing moldy ornaments (assuming I could find them) and an intimidating tangle of burned-out Christmas lights.

Fortunately, the decorating was not nearly as bad as I'd anticipated. Like the root canal you're dreading, only to realize you'd be drugged up beyond caring, the anticipation was worse than the actual task. Somehow I managed to clean and decorate. While I found undiscovered uses for ornaments and heretofore-unheard-of places for lights, the overall effect stopped just short of a Disney display.

Then the event coordinator reminded me that I needed to provide a write-up for the program. "Just a page or two about your style," she said breezily. It certainly sounded benign. After all, I have actually written term papers and an occasional scathing letter to a teacher. Writing is easy, isn't it?

Decorating style? I quickly realized that writer's block is

real, and I'm not even a writer. My parents had a "traditional" home. "Traditional never goes out of style," my mother said. I learned that, while it may not be exciting, modern, or bold, it is practical. I entered adulthood as a "traditional" devotee.

After college, I had my first apartment. Style was not an issue. Of course, if I had to name it, it would be "survival chic." Dumpster diving, yard sales, and creative recycling provided me with lots of inexpensive pieces. It was all about function, not form.

Once I married and had children, style was not all that different. Yes, we had more stuff, but it was the kind of stuff that had to withstand the onslaught of four children in five years. For the uninitiated, the spills and stains that *one* child can visit upon a piece of furniture are staggering, let alone four. We also acquired lots of pieces, mainly in primary colors, that bore a toy maker's logo. I'd apparently moved into my "Little Tikes" chic phase.

As my children grew older, they did become neater. Believe it or not, I actually bought a white couch at one point. Unfortunately, neater is not necessarily neat. The couch did not last long. However, the reality was we were able to start buying nicer things, and our furniture was free from teething and crayon marks. We were getting there.

Then it happened. We were assigned to Italy. Now, I've never cheated on my husband, but I did have a bona fide love affair with Italian furniture. To be completely honest, if furniture was my love affair, then Italian leather, ceramics, fabrics, food, and wine were memorable flings. We definitely did our part to be good Americans and boost the Italian economy.

I spent a lot of time thinking about my style as I wrote my narrative for the tour of homes. I decided that, like everything else in my life, I cannot pigeonhole it. I have been influenced by my parents' warm and traditional home, my yard sale days, my child-proofing days, and my Italian days. I've also lived in ten different states, including Hawaii, and a European country. Over the years, I've seen the homes of people from all along the economic spectrum, some welcoming, some not. The one thing I've taken from all of this is that Army homes are similar.

Regardless of rank or economic status, they are more alike than you'd guess. They all tell a story.

Army homes are almost always comfortable. We have new neighbors to welcome and friends to bid farewell. We have a place for people to visit, to share everything from the mundane to joy and even grief. We have homes that are a tribute to Hawaiian koa wood, Italian inlay, German craftsmanship, and Korean artwork and carving. We tip our hats to the Midwest with antiques, the South with cross-stitched samplers, and the West with hand-thrown pottery. Our homes are a testament to the lives we've led. They carry the remnants and memories of places we've been and friends we've had. Lacking a permanent homebase, our furniture tells the story of our lives. These possessions are not mere pieces. For many of us, they provide the only continuity of our Army years. Yes, they are just material, and in the grand scheme of life, certainly not the most important things. Yet, for the military family, they are the common thread from Fort Lewis to Hawaii, from Fort Bragg to Vicenza, Italy.

As Army people, I don't think we can limit ourselves to a pre-determined style. Whatever you may decide to call your own style, it's always versatile, functional, welcoming, and interesting. Let's call it "Hooah Chic."

ANGELA OWENS is a former Army officer and the spouse of a retired soldier. They live and work in Italy where they enjoy travelling now that they are empty nesters. She is still searching for her perfect decorating style and, of course, the perfect, stain-proof, off-white couch.

December During Deployment

MARNA ASHBURN

Usually in December we haul up our appliance-sized boxes of red bows, garland, table cloths, ornaments, and wreaths from the basement. This year, however, my husband was midway through a 12-month deployment to Afghanistan, and his absence forced me to consider what Yuletide traditions we'd actually observe. With a part-time job and the responsibilities of two children on me, this holiday promised to be more spare than the past. Rather than wrestle 18 years' worth of trimmings up the stairs, I was going to be more selective.

First off, because I knew it would be too depressing to rattle around our house alone during the holidays, my children and I decided to fly to northern California to visit my sisters. They lived within a few minutes of each other and there was a joyful new addition to celebrate, my four-month-old niece Kelly Ann.

In the meantime, "What do you need for it to feel like Christmas around here?" I asked my children after dinner one night. I wanted to establish our essential chords, and then simply let the rest go. In the past, orchestrating all the sights, sounds, and smells of the season fell to me at considerable strain. This year had to be different.

While I assumed a tree was a given, they were indifferent. I thought we might put up a small one early in December, but the idea of cutting a tree, hauling it home, installing it, lighting it, and ornamenting it just made me tired. That's a partner-assisted exercise. Instead, I dropped by the tree farm, and the proprietor graciously gave me armfuls of pine and spruce cuttings for the window boxes and planters of my little Cape-style house. I do love that classic look of evergreen and Christmas red.

And the annual Christmas letter? We military families are sentimental about that verbose narrative. It's our lifeline to each other, the spun gold that keeps us in touch over the years and continents. It pained me when I deleted that task, but because so many in our circle mentioned "Iraq" and "deployments," I'm sure they understood. With a few online clicks, I ordered a photo greeting card and called it done.

Presents were modest this year. My daughter declared she wanted no gifts, just contributions for her study abroad fund. Still, I bought her favorite tea and a calendar of vintage posters. The hefty ski club fee became a large part of my son's gift. My sisters and I, collectively reaching diminishing scale of returns on materialism, agreed not to exchange.

There was a smattering of outings. We strolled down to the local elementary school for the annual craft bazaar, that reassuring slice of Americana with its pipe cleaner snowflakes, themed basket raffles, and second graders singing "Rudolph the Red Nosed Reindeer." At the village Christmas tree lighting, under a cloudless full moon sky, Santa Claus arrived by fire engine while the civic band played carols.

Starting on December 1, we hummed to the holiday CDs stacked in the kitchen and served dinner on special stoneware sponge-painted with snowy evergreens. No doubt we'd make a donation to the food drive and attend a Christmas Eve service. I'll do a little baking—some sugar cookies, perhaps—but certainly not the epic efforts of the past.

As for house decorations, I hung strands of icicle lights inside the windows on suction cup hooks. I bought those when my husband was assigned to Fort Campbell (translation: gone all the time) and I needed something I could put up by myself. I looped the light strand around the hooks and plugged it in. This was *my* essential Christmas chord.

At the end of the day, I sat in the living room with a glass of red wine, turned off the lamps, and enjoyed the enchantment of tiny white lights glowing through curtain sheers. I felt a little sadness, and I wasn't abuzz with that familiar holiday charge, but I also didn't have the exhaustion caused by my self-imposed unrealistic expectations.

Though dad was overseas this year, we looked forward to his two-week leave in January when we'd hang up the "Welcome Home" banner and fill each day to the brim with activities. With that thought, I drained my wine glass, unplugged the white lights, and headed up to bed alone.

MARNA ASHBURN, a U.S. Army Veteran, was an Army wife for twenty years, and is the author of four books about military family life. The most recent one is *Marriage During Deployment: A Memoir of a Military Marriage* (Rowman, 2017). Marna enjoys hiking, biking, sailing, and any outdoor activity with her family. Visit her website at www.HouseholdBaggage.com.

Collecting and Creating Traditions:
Military Holidays are Different
KATHIE HIGHTOWER

My sister and I choose to exchange experiences rather than gifts at the holidays. A few years ago, when our military assignment actually located me only four hours away from her, we agreed to meet halfway for a shared experience. We met in Seattle for a day of department store window shopping, simply to soak up the holiday atmosphere and enjoy each other's company. The highlight of the day was my sister's idea.

"Let's get our photos taken with Santa as a gift for mom," Nancy said. The last photo mom had of us kids sitting on Santa's knee was from many more years ago than I care to admit.

Waiting in line at the Seattle Bon Marché, I noticed that we were the only adults in line without children in tow. To overcome my embarrassment, I started talking to the next woman in line. She was there with her husband and two teenage sons. The photo coordinator interrupted briefly to ask if we wanted to take our photo now or wait until after the short break when a different Santa would be stepping in.

The woman next to me said, "Oh, be sure to wait. He's the best!" It turns out she and her family had been coming to the Bon Marché for the Santa photo for 15 years. "We've had him for the past ten years. He's the most authentic!" she gushed.

I couldn't help but ask, "Do you have all the photos displayed on one wall at Christmas?" Not only at Christmas, but all year long, she answered. Talk about a family tradition!

Of course my immediate thought was, "That's one holiday tradition no military family will ever have!"

I started thinking about our own family holiday traditions and asking other military spouses about theirs.

One favorite Thanksgiving was spent with another military couple. This was before children and we all decided we didn't want to do the big turkey dinner thing that so often just reminded us of the extended family gatherings we were missing.

We drove up to West Virginia from Fort Lee, Virginia, and rented cheap motel rooms in the mountains. Although we did a little hiking even in the rain, we spent most of the time playing raucous games of Pictionary, sharing life stories, and eating the turkey sandwiches I'd made in honor of the day. We all still talk about that as one of the best Thanksgivings ever. Simple but fun.

Everyone I talked with has at least one great memory of a Mess Hall/Dining Facility Thanksgiving meal. My mother-in-law Naomi never stopped talking about the year she joined us at the Fort Lewis dining facility. When she told all her friends that "like President George Bush, I got to spend Thanksgiving eating dinner with the troops," they all replied with envy, "How did you get to do that?!"

Of course, the holidays spent in foreign countries always add a special element.

Three favorites immediately come to mind. One year in Germany a group of military and civil service folks attended an Italian cooking school at a ski hotel in the Dolomites. Because it was the very first week the hotel was open for the season and because Italians never traveled there until the day after Christmas, we got very inexpensive rates and unbelievable service as they trained the new staff. I think there was more staff in the hotel than guests! Our group's white elephant gift exchange was enough of a nod to the holiday for all of us.

I can't think of any more magical place to be at Christmas than in Germany at one of the many Christmas markets. Our favorite was in the old, small-walled city of Bad Wimpfen: light snow falling, the smell of spiced *gluhwein* (hot spiced wine), and *lebkuchen* (German gingerbread often shaped like hearts with words etched in icing) and all the fun nutcrackers, wood carvings and other interesting gifts to consider. We each enjoyed a *warme seele* (warm soul) which is a great combination of ham and melted Swiss cheese in a fresh baguette, as good as its name implies.

We spent New Year's Eve or *Silvesterabend* with another

military family at our German neighbor's house. We all "read our fortunes" by melting little pewter figures in a spoon over a candle and then dropping them into cold water to see what shape emerged. Everyone, including the kids, danced into the wee hours of the morning. We welcomed the New Year with sparklers and champagne and cider. And we still remember how intrigued we were by the question our German friends asked us as we all stood outside in the cold watching the town fireworks. It wasn't, "What are your New Year's resolutions?" Instead they wanted to know, "Are you satisfied with last year?"

Another holiday "tradition" that military spouses always bring up is that of "creating a new extended family" wherever you are stationed. By joining with other military families and inviting any single military or civilian workers to join in, holiday gatherings can be just as rich and interesting as with your own extended family, and sometimes even more so.

In fact I laughed this year when a civilian couple I know told me they chose to go to a hotel in a town an hour away from home, "just to avoid one more year of too much family togetherness at the holidays." Not all gatherings, as we know, are Norman Rockwell ones.

Do any memories of holidays with our real extended families stand out? Of course they do, but I think they stand out even more strongly because they don't happen every year. When we do get together, we all recognize how rare and special that gathering is.

For most military families, there is at least one holiday that is remembered either because it was celebrated before or after the real holiday due to a deployment.

"One Easter that stands out in my memory," says my friend Holly, "is the one when the Easter egg hunt and Easter brunch at my house was women and children only. All the male spouses were deployed."

With the current longer deployments in Iraq and Afghanistan, many families are missing every holiday with their military member. For many of them, holiday photos show family gatherings with a "Flat Daddy" or "Flat Mommy" standing in for their military member for that moment as a way to feel more connected.

One of these days I'm going to get around to making a collage of photos from the wide variety of memorable holiday experiences we've had over the years of our military life.

Somehow I think that collage will be a little richer, at least to me, than a wall of photos with the same Bon Marché Santa every year. Both great family traditions ... only different!

KATHIE HIGHTOWER is an accomplished author, columnist, and international speaker, who retired as an Army Reserve lieutenant colonel after 26 years of service. She and co-author Holly Scherer created and presented "Follow Your Dreams While You Follow the Military"™ workshops all over the United States, Europe, and Japan. The information provided in this three-hour workshop was expanded into the book *Military Spouse Journey: Discover the Possibilities & Live Your Dreams* (Elva Resa Publishing). For information, visit www.elvaresa.com.

Moving On

A Loud Silence
SUZIE TROTTER

Transitioning out of the Navy should be an easy thing. It was something we wanted. We had planned for it. We were prepared and excited to make the move. Why, then, was it so strange and difficult? Why did we feel empty and uneasy when we began our civilian life after the military?

From a bystander's view, it looked like we had everything. We were high school crushes married right after college, and we were a fun-loving couple. My husband is an adventurous, good-looking, successful oral surgeon. He married me, a youthful, spirited registered nurse. We traveled the world with the Navy, making six moves in 13 years, two of them overseas. We survived Hurricane Hugo while at Parris Island and seven typhoons on Guam. We ate pickled kimchi in Korea and Turkish Delight in Istanbul. Swam with the sharks in the crystal blue waters of Palau and shared bintu lunch boxes on its white, sandy rock islands. We named our own island off of Crete and toured Europe with great friends. Three tours in Virginia grounded us and we fell in love with the flora and fauna of the state. We decided to make it our permanent home in 2001.

The timing was perfect. Our son, Bradley, was ready to enroll in high school. He had a harder time adjusting with each successive move, and we desired some permanency so he'd be able to complete high school without moving again. And my husband, Brad, was eager to launch into private practice. So we made the leap and decided to end our active duty life after 13 years of service. We were far, though, from having everything. We were really just beginning.

There was something about working for a "company" for 13 years and just quitting that didn't sit right with me. I discussed with Brad all he'd invested into the Navy and how it would be worth seeking options for retirement if possible. So we decided he would stay in the Reserves until we were solidly on our feet in our new civilian life, instead of simply walking away and terminating military service. Truly, that was the best decision we made in our transition. Being new to a community, it was crucial to feel connected and secure during the stressful changes. We could still shop in the commissary at nearby Fort Lee, go to the chapel, utilize our military ID, and have the familiar DOD sticker on our car, comforting symbols and actions that cushioned the uneasiness in our new civilian way of life.

We built a lovely house in a good neighborhood near Richmond, Virginia. Brad partnered in a group oral surgery practice. Things were falling into place just as we'd planned and researched and dreamed. But with all that, there was an eerie silence present. As a family in a military community, the common bond was the unique difference each member brought to the local command. But I soon felt that our differences were obstacles to assimilating into an established community. The phones didn't ring and the traditional dinners and social invitations didn't come as automatically as they did in military life.

I remember the first snowfall in our new house and how magical it was for me and our children. We looked out the back window in wonderment. As we gazed, we saw the neighbor's children pass through the backyard with sleds and meet up with five other neighborhood children. I could see the sadness in my daughter's eyes as she wished she had been invited. We had lived there for six months, and I found it interesting that after the first hellos, the neighbors kept to their same routines. In the military, the first hello was followed by the first dinner invitation, followed by continuous communication. It began the minute we checked into command. Our sponsor got us settled and connected with our surroundings, activities, and social life—instant friends and family.

In civilian life, we had to work a lot harder to be accepted and included. We were met with suspicion by folks who'd lived in the area their whole lives because of our different background and history. We didn't know how much to share as most of what we had to say about our life and experiences was not the typical jaunt to Myrtle Beach for spring break. So we kept quiet about ourselves and asked more about them. I silenced myself in order to earn trust and friendship. But was it real friendship if I couldn't reveal my true self?

I began working at the local health department and had the privilege of meeting many employees in the county complex. I soon met the supervisor in Environmental Health, Frank, who was retired Army and had lived in Germany during his career. I briefly shared my experiences as a Navy wife, and in that moment the silence lifted. It was a relief to find a kindred spirit with similar experiences, and I no longer felt different. And we didn't even say much. We instantly had a common bond and were connected through our shared military understanding. We exchanged stories and laughter and to this day, I enjoy my conversations with "Chief Scherra," the warrant officer who was committed to his career, his shop, and his country.

I continued to meet others as I grew into my role at work. Another nurse lived in Hawaii back in her military spouse days. There were some military brats who shared some of their memories. I met a gentleman at a training seminar who spent time on Guam back in the day. We didn't really say much. We just introduced ourselves and then pretty much sat in silence. But I was comforted by that silence. There was an understanding of common experiences and military traditions. The people I met made my world brighter and more vibrant.

As for the children, they too were finding their home. One girl in my daughter's class was born in Germany, so she no longer felt like she stood out as "the girl born on Guam." Social media websites like Facebook have opened up their world all the more to lost friends from past duty stations. Now they can talk whenever they like online and be connected as if they've never been apart. Our son graduated from high school last spring and is enjoying his new home as a freshman in college.

After five years since leaving active duty, I feel now like I usually did after six months or so at a new duty station. I feel like I'm finally part of the community. But it has taken a lot of work and a lot of silence. Our connections with the military have been the stabilizing force. Both my husband's success in the Reserves and the common bonds we have with prior military and those currently serving have supported us as we built relationships in our new community. We look forward to my husband's retirement as a Captain from the Navy Dental Corps Reserves in three years. It will be a jubilant celebration, and we will be filled with gratitude for all of our family, friends, neighbors, and military family. The silence is broken. We are home.

Currently living on the Chesapeake Bay with her husband in Hampton, Virginia, SUZIE TROTTER enjoys all things water. She crews for women's sailing races, cruises with her husband on their sailboat, and volunteers on whale education boat tours for the Virginia Marine Science Museum and Aquarium. Their empty nest still fills with her daughter and son, along with family and friends who enjoy sharing in bayfront living. Follow her travel and foodie adventures on Instagram, @suzietrotter.

Missing It
MARY CORNELL

Since my husband Keith retired from the Army in 2000 after 23 years in the service, we've stayed in one place. We have a spacious home with a backyard pool. I have a job I like, and we've made friends in the area. My oldest daughter, who has special needs, has thrived with the consistently good care she's received here. My other two children love staying in one place with the same friends. Every day I wake up and think I have a great life.

Yet twice a month I travel 45 minutes to the nearest commissary and not only get my shopping done, I get my "military fix," too. I flash my military ID and drive through the security gate just like old times. I get a big kick out of it.

You see, I *loved* being a military family member—absolutely adored it. Now that we are established in a civilian community, I miss military life. I miss all the pomp, like the parades and changes of command. I miss seeing folks in uniform. I miss the discipline and structure. It's a lot like having a baby; I remember all the good stuff but forgot the bad stuff.

When Keith was in the Army, I liked traveling and meeting new people. We lived in a lot of great places like Panama and Washington State (spectacular views of Mount Ranier and lots of outdoor activities), but my favorite place was Germany. It was such a clean and beautiful country and the locals were so nice. I loved walking in the Christmas markets with a mug of hot spiced wine. We were stationed with a terrific bunch of people there. I remember one New Year's Eve we were all at a party and I said, "Why don't we have a barbecue tomorrow?" So on January 1, about 50 of us set up grills and tables and burn barrels to keep warm and had a spontaneous New Year's cookout in the ten degree weather. That was the kind of group we had. What a good memory. Even now I keep trying to get Keith to go back to Germany, but it hasn't worked out.

I miss the camaraderie of Army life. Women from so many

diverse backgrounds—all friends—took care of each other. We were in the same boat: stationed overseas far from family, husband gone, kids sick. We've all done it. I'll never find that anywhere else. I miss the instant connection with other women. I could meet any military spouse and chat like old friends. It's automatic acceptance. How nice is that? It's a club and you're a member of it.

I miss the collective identity. I miss the sense of belonging to a larger group with a shared mission. In my neighborhood, we don't have much in common with the people around us except we all live in the same area. We have a good social connection now but even that took a while.

I miss the shorthand communication in the Army. Acronyms and lingo were second nature and everybody spoke them. When we first retired, I still used military terms a lot and people looked at me strangely. Then I realized, "Oh yeah, you don't know what a Class VI store is." After I stopped using the military slang, I had a lot less explaining to do.

Back in the Army, people just understood what you meant. Since my husband was in Special Forces, when he left I didn't know where he was or when he'd be back. Try telling that to a civilian. They'll think you're insane. "What kind of life is that?" they'd wonder. But military friends understand.

I also miss the separations and the reunions of military life. It was okay when Keith left and really nice when he came home. I learned I could take care of myself. It was great for growth and self-reliance. I'm not afraid to ask for help now. Part of that comes from my personality; the military had something to do with the rest.

I miss not getting rid of junk. With every move we cleaned out our closets. I've lived here longer than anywhere else since we got married and we've accumulated so much stuff. When we were an active duty family, if a box didn't get opened between moves, it got tossed. We obviously didn't need what was in it. I'm itching to move now and when our youngest graduates from high school next year, that's probably what we'll do.

Whenever Keith came home with news of the next active

duty assignment, I thought, "Great! We're off on another adventure!" That's also how I felt when he told me he was ready to retire. I was okay with it.

But I'd be lying if I didn't admit I miss the people and the close-knit community. I liked doing something new and exciting every two years. Somebody once asked me what I missed about Army life and my daughter piped up, "She misses everything!"

The military life we led helped me grow as a person. Each of the different friendships and experiences over the years made me who I am today and brought me to this place. And I have to admit, it's a pretty great place.

MARY CORNELL met Keith during college when they were in ROTC together, and they've now been married 37 years. She likes playing softball, bowling, reading, and relaxing in her backyard with Keith.

Yes, Virginia, There Is an Afterlife
JOAN BROWN

"Out, out in the cold, cold world" was the mantra I chanted, along with the rest of my class about our upcoming graduation from a school we'd all come to love. As impatient as we were for our independence, we also knew we'd feel the shock of leaving the warmth of a nest we'd feathered with friends during our years together.

Leaving the military can feel a lot like that, even for those of us who, early on, trudged along only to be with the one we loved. Some wives actually have a harder time adjusting to retirement than their husbands. For them, it goes beyond, "For better or worse, but not for lunch," or him trying to alphabetize the pantry.

When my husband Don was preparing to retire from the Air Force after 32 years, friends did me the favor of asking, "Now that you can do anything you want, what do you think you'll do?" It gave me pause and made me think about the dream I'd once had of being a writer, a published writer.

But first there were all the decisions about where we were going to live, both temporarily and permanently, now that no one was ordering us somewhere. And what on earth was Don going to do? When he finally decided he could work from home in Washington State, a place we loved and where we already had friends, our move there helped us immerse ourselves faster in both the civilian and nearby military communities.

For us, keeping one foot planted in both the civilian and military worlds has been the key to happiness in retirement. Air Force people talk of "opening the hangar doors" when the conversation turns to flying, but always living in the past doesn't foster learning new things or meeting new friends. A new life also shifts the focus well beyond the base or post.

Others think of "moving on" as a chance to blot out the service part of their lives as if it never existed. But that would mean forgetting all those friendships we cherish, all the people who become more "family" than our blood relatives.

Keeping in touch with that far-flung brood takes work, but it's a labor that pays joyful dividends. Writing cards at holiday time, remembering birthdays, traveling to visit or hosting get-togethers, sending emails or calling on the phone all take time and effort. But they reward us with a richer life.

Many retired military spouses I know have gone on to pursue their dreams. One has done wonderfully with her "Dress for Success" program to help women enter the workforce. Others have soared in the art world, winning great acclaim for their work. Then there's the investment counselor, the friend who not only sold real estate but rehabbed houses, or the wife who went to law school and became an expert on elder law. Many remark on their delight in being able to build a business without having to start over every few years at a new location.

I'd been an English major and teacher, but pursuing my goal of being published was little more than a pipe dream. Then I saw a blurb in our local newspaper about a writing seminar offered nearby. There I met Lee Roddy, whose novel *The Life and Times of Grizzly Adams* became a prime-time television show on NBC. He suggested I attend a writer's camp that summer in order to learn how to sell my work.

I took his advice, went to camp, and came home elated, sure I could now do it. The next weekend I met a glass artist who specialized in restoring cathedral windows. After interviewing her and taking photographs of her work, I sent out a query letter to a local magazine. The idea was turned down. Discouraged, I rationalized that I was in the throes of moving and too busy with a new community to send out anything else and risk further rejection.

A few months later the artist asked me what had happened with the story. Guilty about dropping the ball, I returned to work, choosing more carefully where I sent the next query letter. Much to my surprise, I soon got a "Yes" from the magazine section of the *Cincinnati Enquirer* and was asked to do an article "on spec." If they liked what I submitted, they'd buy it.

I wrote it, they liked it, and they bought it. I framed that first check for a published article. But I still dragged my feet about sending out queries; who wants to be rejected? In the next three years, I'd published only three articles. Then Don upped the ante. "You have to earn a profit with your writing this year," he said. "I claimed your start-up costs on our income tax, and the IRS says you have to earn a profit three out of every five years, or it's considered a hobby and not deductible."

It was all the motivation I needed. I got busy and sent out queries, whether it meant rejection or not. Hard work and patience paid off and now, 200 published articles and two books later, I'm still fascinated by the process of researching non-fiction. It's like being a student again or sharing life with people from all over the world, learning new ways of cooking and doing things, as Don and I and our three children did all those years that we frequently found ourselves transplanted somewhere new.

Are there things I miss about this post-service way of life? Sure, I can't live near enough to all of the dear friends I've made. Pack rat that I am, I could use the motivation of a looming move to force me to get rid of stuff. But I'd rather not have to do the real move, thank you very much.

For years I squirreled away the most significant of our packing boxes, like the ones for the stereo, as "insurance," sort of like saving the crib and other baby things, just in case. But the boxes are long gone now and so, I hope, is moving. Travel provides an exciting substitute

When the time finally comes to retire from the military, some of the best things in life are still to come. Yes, Virginia, there is an afterlife and it's feathered with friends, both old and new, things to learn and do, and fresh ways to help make even a "cold, cold" world a much warmer one.

JOAN BROWN became a freelance writer after thirty-two years as an Air Force wife. She is the author of over 200 articles which have appeared in such regional and national publications as *U.S. Air Magazine, Woman's World, Seattle Magazine* and numerous newspapers. She is also the co-author of *Colors of France: A Painting Pilgrimage* with artist and fellow Air Force wife Margaret Hoybach. Her second book, *Move—And Other Four-Letter Words*, a memoir of her life as a military wife and mother of three, won Honorable Mention for Biography in the 8th Annual DIY Book Festival Competition. Read more at www.hearthlandpublishing.com.

Gratitude

My hearty appreciation to the following folks who made this book possible.

The contributors opened their hearts and expressed their personal military moments. Sharing your humanity is a brave and generous act. Thanks for joining me in this effort to offer others a glimpse of our world.

Artist Julie Negron, Air Force wife and creator of "Jennyspouse" comic strip, who put her amazing talent to work on the interior illustrations and the cover of the first edition.

Nancy Cleary and Wyatt-MacKenzie Publishing once again believed in hearing the story from the perspective of the military spouse.

Dr. Nedra Reynolds and Lisa Magnuson offered thoughtful critiques of the manuscript.

Bob Gulla: proofreader, sounding board, and friend.

My family, as always.

Julie Negron created the *Stars & Stripes* Sunday comic strip, *Jenny, the Military Spouse*. A lifelong Air Force brat who has lived all over the world—the Philippines, Japan, Taiwan, Germany, Alaska, and across the United States—Julie has been drawing and attending art courses since she could hold a pencil, receiving further training through commercial art and multimedia graphics studies in Colorado and South Carolina. Her professional career began in the late 80s with a job as an editorial cartoonist in Oregon. Julie eventually returned to her military roots when she married Angel Negron, a pilot in the U.S. Air Force. Because of frequent moves, she continued her career as a freelance illustrator and worked on everything from official military publications to marketing campaign spots and posters to training manuals for Human Resources departments. In 1999, Julie opened her own graphic arts studio where she created brochures, advertisements, websites, and magazine illustrations for local clients. She also taught adult art classes at the local community center. She and her husband moved to Peachtree City, Georgia, when he retired from the Air Force.